STEVE

MARRY M

CMY

LUCKNOW

Lucknow

A city between cultures

edited by

MALVIKA SINGH

ACADEMIC FOUNDATION
NEW DELHI

www.academicfoundation.com

First published in 2011
by

ACADEMIC FOUNDATION
4772-73 / 23 Bharat Ram Road, (23 Ansari Road),
Darya Ganj, New Delhi - 110 002 (India).
Phones : 23245001 / 02 / 03 / 04.
Fax : +91-11-23245005.
E-mail : books@academicfoundation.com
www. academicfoundation.com

Cataloging in Publication Data--DK
  Courtesy: D.K. Agencies (P) Ltd. <docinfo@dkagencies.com>

Lucknow : a city between cultures / edited by Malvika Singh.
    p.   cm.
  ISBN 13: 9788171888894
  ISBN 10: 8171888895

1. Lucknow (India)--Civilization.   I. Singh, Malvika.

DDC 954.2   22

Typeset by Italics India, New Delhi.
Printed and bound in India.

For

HAMIDA HABIBULLAH

Contents

Introduction

MALVIKA SINGH

The journal SEMINAR turned fifty in the year 2009. At that time we decided to bring out themed 'compendiums' from the vast treasure of material that the monthly had published over the five and more, decades. As part of that ongoing project, Academic Foundation have reproduced six special issues of SEMINAR, as a set of individual books, that celebrate the historic and famed cities of Delhi; Bombay, now Mumbai; Calcutta, now Kolkata; Madras, now Chennai; Hyderabad and Lucknow. We are delighted that this work will be accessible to a wider audience of Indians as well as visitors to India, who would want to share and experience the many special, personal and individual insights into the life and times of these cities, based on memories, on hitherto unspoken behind-the-scenes stories, some full of joy and others that lament the change, all of which are woven together in an extraordinary tapestry.

My gratitude to Rituraj and Sanu Kapila for having recognised the merit of these carefully crafted mini compendiums, and for reproducing them with much care. My thanks to all the writers who participated in the issues of SEMINAR, making them lively, unusual and substantive. To my colleagues at SEMINAR, my sincere thanks for supporting the many SEMINAR related 'ventures' like this one!

A city between cultures

HARSH SETHI

MORE than any other North Indian city, Lucknow in popular imagination and in cinematic and literary texts, has been identified as a city of languorous grace, of *adab* and *tehzeeb*. Chosen as the capital by the Shia Nawabs of Faizabad in the sunset years of the Mughal Raj, in less than a century the seat of Awadh power gained fame as the Venice of the Orient, a city whose buildings and palaces, art and craft, cuisine, courtly manners, even the conversational style and language, set it apart, marking a standard for all to admire and emulate.

Even the unseating of the last Nawab, Wajid Ali Shah, by the East India Company in the 1850s, or the sacking of the city by English troops following the failed 'revolt' of 1857, despite wreaking widespread destruction failed to destroy the unique culture of Lucknow. Sustained in part by the *taluqdars* of Awadh as also the memories of past glory, Lucknow retained its pride of place as a unique amalgam of Ganga-Jamuna culture. To the fabled Imambaras and Qaisarbagh and the vitality of the Chowk, the British added Hazratganj, a superior version of the Civil Lines that they had contributed to many other cities.

Despite being a centre of erstwhile Muslim nobility and an important seat of emerging Muslim League politics in the 1930s and '40s, Lucknow never quite became a breeding ground for religious obscurantism. In part this may have to do with the Shia influence, a sect whose rituals and practices the majority Hindu populace seemed more comfortable with. It is often remarked that the Urdu of Lucknow is 'softer' than that of Aligarh, arguably an influence of the religious poetry credited to the many Sufi saints of the region as also the *marsiyas* sung during Muharram. Not only were the Imambaras open to all, people of diverse faiths and persuasions participated in the Muharram processions. What also helped was the regard and fondness with which the citizenry remembered not only Wajid Ali but Begum Hazrat Mahal and her role in the 1857 uprising.

Equally important was the role of the Congress and the Left in promoting their version of a syncretic culture, helped in no small measure by Muslim comrades articulating a worldview distinct from their co-religionists from Aligarh, the other great centre of Muslim learning. Not to be underestimated was the role of educational centres like Lucknow University and the King George Medical College, for long crucial sites for intellectual discourse.

If 1857 had dealt one blow to the city, the Partition of 1947 was another, as many among the erstwhile Muslim elite chose Pakistan over secular India. In many ways the city found it difficult to recover from the loss of a crucial section of its elite and leadership, leaving the large mass of its Muslim populace rudderless. And as Lucknow became the seat of political and administrative power of modern India's largest state, Uttar Pradesh, attracting new resources and people wedded to new cultural and social norms, the Muslims of the city became further ghettoized. The Lucknow of the nawabs and taluqdars now survived only as memory.

The change, however, was gradual. For the first two decades of post-independence India, Lucknow was still a city of charm. Probably, the politics of the Nehru years was not as all-consuming. The university boasted of great dons like D.P. Mukherjee and Radhakamal

Mukherjee, the left-wing economist, V.B. Singh and the brilliant but eccentric sociologist, A.K. Saran, to name just a few. The medical college was counted as amongst the best in the country. And the science labs like the Central Drug Research Institute attracted brilliant researchers. Playing a crucial role were the *mushairas* and *qawwali* sessions, as also a theatrical tradition strongly influenced by the cultural activism of the IPTA (Indian People's Theatre Association).

The cuisine continued to be delectable and visitors, in particular those favouring animal protein, invariably made a beeline to the famed *tunda* and *galauti* kebabs of the Chowk. An evening stroll at Hazratganj was a must, as was buying *chikan kurtas*. And if the Muslim socials of Bombay cinema are any indication, Lucknow was still steeped in the culture of the old. Even its courtesans were seen as a class apart from their less fortunate sisters elsewhere – repositories of *ghazal gayaki* and *kathak*.

In fact, so hegemonic is this representation that even the creative output of litterateures like Rangheya Raghav, Amritlal Nagar or Shivani have failed to de-centre the imagery of Lucknow as a centre of Muslim culture, this despite Hindus forming the vast majority of the populace. Though not quite the *huzun* that Orhan Pamuk claims Istanbul is suffused with, representations of Lucknow continue to be marked by both nostalgia and a sense of loss. Little surprise, more recent renditions foreground not just the lack of soul but the emergence of a public culture with few saving graces.

Like the region of which it is a part, the city of Lucknow has witnessed tumultuous, some would say calamitous, changes in the last few decades. As politics transformed from the less fiercely contested days of Congress dominance and new social groups staked their claims on state power and resources, the city too lost its cohesiveness. For a start, Lucknow was never an industrial city. Attracting resources primarily as a seat of political power, it drew in the new entrepreneurs – the contractors, middlemen and builders seeking their cut of public resources. Fractious politics consumed all – the institutions, public spaces and buildings, and public culture. If the Lucknow of yesteryears was epitomized by films like *Umrao Jaan* and *Pakeezah*, its present is captured in gritty films like *Seher*, a story of mafia and politics and the losing battle to contain growing criminality. And little epitomizes this shift better than the many stories about the goings-on in Darul Shafa, the MLAs hostel, or the proceedings in the state assembly, not to forget the need for permanent presence of armed police pickets on the university campus.

Like all such representations, the Lucknow of old and of contemporary times, is part myth – the city invariably being far more complex than the fictionalized accounts might suggest. Unfortunately, we have far too few social histories or accounts of everyday life in this large urban centre to easily challenge dominant myths. A city, after all, is more than the lifestyle of its elite. And while it is rarely easy to admire the new makers of the city's destiny, both the emerging subaltern politicians and the realty giants like the Sahara group, their impact on the making of the new city needs documentation and analysis. No matter how glorious the past may appear, it is to the future that we must turn, even if it today appears garish.

Much will depend upon how the new ruling party, the BSP, and the new Chief Minister, Mayawati, shape politics in the state and thereby mould the city. What the residents of Lucknow look forward to, other than the sprucing up of the Ambedkar Park and the addition of new statues of Dalit icons, is an improvement in law and order. Maybe then the city will recover its lost elan and strolling down Hazratganj will once again become a pleasure.

This volume seeks to provide some vignettes of a remarkable city and its struggle to reinvent itself.

A study of a dying culture

RUDRANGSHU MUKHERJEE

THE independent principality of Awadh was established in 1722 by an Iranian adventurer called Saadat Ali Khan who refused the imperial order transferring him to Malwa and made Lucknow the seat of his power. Awadh remained an independent entity till 7 February 1856 when Lord Dalhousie annexed it to the British Empire in India. Earlier, in 1801, Lord Wellesley had truncated the province. Despite the truncation, Awadh when it was annexed held an area of 23,923 square miles with a population of 5,000,000 and yielded to the British government revenue of £1,300,000. But what was more important than these dry-as-dust figures of area, demography and revenue was the fact that from the second half of the 18th century to the time Awadh was annexed, Lucknow, the capital city, had emerged as a great centre of cultural refinement and sophistication. Lucknow set the standards of *adab* and taste in matters of music, food, dress and so on.

Culture in Lucknow flourished because of the patronage it received from successive nawabs and kings and from their courts. Big landholders, known in Awadh as taluqdars, replicated the styles of the royal court in their own palaces and forts, albeit on a lower scale than the court. Life in Lucknow became famous for its luxury and its pleasures. It also became synonymous with decadence and debauchery. But critics of this pursuit of pleasure and conspicuous consumption overlooked the historical context that induced this lifestyle.

One of the conditions of the independence of Awadh in an era when the British were expanding their dominions all over India was the acceptance of British indirect control by the rulers of Awadh. Through what the British came to call subsidiary alliance, the British stationed a Resident and troops in Lucknow, and made the nawabs pay for them. The troops were supposed to protect Awadh and the Resident controlled the government, though the responsibility of running the administration remained with the nawab. At frequent intervals, the British escalated the amount needed to maintain the troops, the price for independence. Two important consequences followed. One was the fact that Awadh was drained of resources. The other reason was that the arrangement placed the rulers of Awadh in a bizarre situation: they had responsibility without power. The real power vested with the Resident who curbed any initiative that the nawab showed for governance.

The historian T.R. Metcalf has provided an apposite description of the plight of the Awadh nawabs:

'With the subsidiary allowance drawn tightly around him, he could not ignore the British and act as before. But he had neither the training nor the military force to act upon the injunction of his European advisers. So the nawabs who succeeded Sadaat Ali Khan, one after the other, increasingly abandoned the attempt to govern and retired into the *zenana*, where they amused themselves with wine, women and poetry. The sensuous life did not reflect sheer perversity or weakness of character on the part of the nawabs. Indolence was rather the only appropriate response to the situation in which the princes of Awadh were placed.'

This situation was only one aspect of the misgovernment in Awadh. The other point mentioned above was equally important. The British presence in Awadh directly and indirectly drained the region of its resources. The British kept hiking their demands on the Awadh rulers for the upkeep of the troops in Lucknow. There was also the fact of British trade which caused economic drain and dislocation. Since 1765 trade controlled by the English East India Company and by European private merchants had channeled economic resources away from Awadh. This had eroded the very viability of the Awadh administration, leading to misgovernment, which in turn had become the reason first for its truncation in 1801 and then its eventual annexation in 1856.

The historian Peter Reeves has noted that Awadh was important to the British, not for what it could do but for what it had to offer. No wonder that British administrators often saw Awadh as something that could be eaten. Lord Wellesley had promised London, 'a supper of Oudh'; and Lord Dalhousie had described Awadh as 'a cherry which will drop into our mouths some day. It has long been ripening.'

The culture and refinement of Lucknow in the late 18th and early 19th centuries should be viewed against this backdrop. One of the greatest achievements of Indo-Islamic culture occurred with the threat of a British takeover looming over it. The great and the good of Lucknow – the *raees* of the city – went about their business with the full knowledge that the British Resident was peering over their shoulders with suspicious and disapproving eyes.

We are fortunate that there exists a vivid depiction of the culture of Lucknow in its best, and alas its last years. This is available in Abdul Halim Sharar, *Lucknow: The Last Phase of an Oriental Culture*, a collection of vignettes of Lucknow that were published originally in Urdu from 1913 onwards in the Lucknow journal *Dil Gudaz*. The series when it first appeared was called *Hindustan Men Mashriqi Tamaddun ka Akhri Namuna* (literally, the last example of an oriental culture in India).

The life that Sharar described was that of the affluent. It was a life of leisure, gracious and luxurious, enjoyed by a group of people who did not care about their source of wealth. It was a world of patronage that spread downwards from the nawab to the nobility to the landholders. The lifestyle supported an enormous body of retainers: servants, artisans, singers, musicians and so on. A network of dependence held it together.

Sharar's book provides details of the kind of activities that engaged the upper classes of Lucknow. One of the principal concerns was refinement of etiquette that spread from how one dressed, to how one greeted a peer or an elder or someone higher in status, to how one ate, to how one chewed *paan*. All aspects of behaviour were guided by a code of rituals. The lack of knowledge of the code or a transgression of the code was enough to make one an outcast. Lucknow was famous for its adab and its graciousness. Leisure centred around activities like kite flying, cock fighting, eating and, of course, poetry and music.

The spirit of this culture can perhaps be illustrated through two incidents. In 1784, there was a severe famine in Awadh. The then nawab, Asaf ud Daula did not want to inflict the indignity of charity on his subjects. So he undertook the project of building the Imam Bara to alleviate the sufferings of the population. The people who worked to build it were given food in return. It was said that the famine was so severe that even the rich were starving. To feed them, the nawab arranged for the construction work to be carried on at night. The gentry came under cover of darkness, worked by torchlight and got their food.

The other incident comes from the reign of Wajid Ali Shah, the last king of Awadh. He was very fond of music and even wrote his own operas. He was so impressed by the rahas relating to the life of Krishna that he composed one himself and then played the role of Krishna in it. Wajid Ali Shah made an attempt to rule. He formed cavalry regiments to which he gave poetic names like Banka, Dandy, Tircha, Fop, Ghangaur, Dark. His infantry regiments bore the names Akhtari, Lucky, Nadiri and Rare. But the Resident stopped his activities and so he retreated completely into his music and a life of leisure.

The people of Lucknow loved the songs he wrote and sang them all the time. When the British asked him to sign a treaty handing over the administration to the English East India Company, he refused to sign. Wajid Ali ordered his subjects not to oppose the British annexation of Awadh when he came to know that many of them were ready to resist. Wajid Ali was exiled to Metia Burz in Calcutta. When he left his beloved Lucknow, the people recited *nanha* (dirges) and followed him all the way to Kanpur. A song of the period said, 'Noble and peasant all wept together/ and all the world wept and wailed/Alas! The chief has bidden adieu to/ his country and gone abroad.'

A contemporary noted: 'The condition of this town [Lucknow] without any exaggeration was such that it appeared that on the departure of Jan-I Alam [as Wajid Ali was fondly known], the life has gone out of the body, and the body of this town had been left lifeless... there was no street or market and house which did not wail out the cry of agony in separation of Jan-I Alam.'

There was no doubt in the minds of the people about who was responsible for the plight of their beloved king. A folk song of the time lamented, '*Angrez Bahadur ain: mulk lain linho*' – the honourable English came and took the country.

But the annexation was not the end of Lucknow's *ancien* regime. The end came through an even more tumultuous event, the revolt of 1857. The revolt in Awadh began with the mutiny of the Lucknow garrison on the evening of 30th May. The mutiny spread swiftly to the cantonments in the districts. In Lucknow, faced with the destruction, plunder and killings that the sepoys perpetrated, the British under Henry Lawrence took refuge in the Residency. Once British authority in the districts of Awadh had collapsed, sepoys from there began to pour into Lucknow. Taluqdars and their retainers joined them. The attitude of the taluqdars is best illustrated by what Hanwant Singh, the Raja of Kalakankar, told Captain Barrow who he had saved from the wrath of the sepoys. He said:

'Sahib, your countryman came into this country and drove out our king. You sent your officers round the districts to examine the titles to the estates. At one blow you took from me lands which from time immemorial had been in my family. I submitted. Suddenly misfortune fell upon you. The people of the land rose against you. You came to me whom you had despoiled. I have saved you. But now, I march at the head of my retainers to Lakhnao to try and drive you from the country.'

With the arrival of men from the districts, the battle to completely oust the British from Lucknow began. On the one hand, there was fierce fighting around the Residency. On the other hand, there were scenes of great rejoicing in the city. The rebels went around in groups crying *Bom Mahadeo* and distributed sweets. They declared Birjis Qadr, the young prince, to be the King of Awadh with his mother Begum Hazrat Mahal as the regent. They called Birjis Qadr, embraced him and said, 'You are Kanhaiya', harking back perhaps to Wajid Ali playing Krishna in a *raha*.

British troops under Outram and Havelock entered the Residency on 25th September 1857 but this offered no relief since their supply lines were cut off as rebels surrounded them. Every overture made to the rebel leadership for negotiations were spurned. Around the time when Colin Campbell's relief force was trying to enter Lucknow, there were more than 50,000 men defending the city. This number increased when Campbell's forces evacuated the British from Lucknow. The frenzy of the rebels was enhanced by the arrival of Maulavi Ahmadullah Shah who claimed to have received divine orders to throw the British out of India. It was only when Campbell re-entered the city in March 1858 that the revolt in Lucknow was finally quelled and the rebels dispersed into the countryside to carry on their resistance there.

The aftermath of Campbell's conquest of Lucknow brought the curtain down on the culture and the ambience of the city. The British troops were given a free rein to sack the city and they went berserk. For a few days, the British army had ceased to be an army at all. William Howard Russell, the correspondent of *The Times* witnessed the loot and the plunder:

'The scene of plunder was indescribable. The soldiers had broken up several of the store-rooms, and pitched the contents into the court, which was lumbered with cases, with embroidered clothes, gold and silver brocade, silver vessels, arms, banners, drums, shawls, scarfs, musical instruments, mirrors, pictures, books, accounts, medicine bottles, gorgeous standards, shields, spears, and a heap of things... Through these moved the men, wild with excitement, "drunk with plunder". I had often heard the phrase, but never saw the thing itself before. They smashed to pieces the fowling-pieces and pistols to get at the gold mountings and the stones set in the stocks. They burned in a fire, which they made in the centre of the court, brocades and embroidered shawls for the sake of the gold and silver. China, glass, and jade they dashed to pieces in pure wantonness; pictures they ripped up, or tossed on the flames; furniture shared the same fate.'

One estimate said that the loot from Lucknow amounted to a million and a quarter sterling. To quote Russell again:

'There are companies which can boast of privates with thousands of pounds worth in their ranks. One man I heard of who complacently offered to lend an officer "whatever sum he wanted if he wished to buy over the Captain". Others have remitted large sums to their friends. Ere this letter reaches England, many a diamond, emerald and delicate pearl will have told its tale in a very quiet pleasant way, of the storm and the sack of Kaiserbagh.'

Amidst such scenes, the graciousness of Lucknow passed into history to make way for colonial modernity.

The monuments, the makers, the real city

ROSIE LLEWELLYN-JONES

LUCKNOW – 'City of Vice and Roses' as a British writer described it earlier this year, or 'the last memento of Mughal culture' as Maulana Sharar called it in the 1920s. Somewhere between the well-trodden clichés on the tawdry glitter of the Nawabi Court and the cosy view of a Mughal fly trapped in colonial amber lies the real city, greatly changed both by Indians and Britons – lively, carefree and a thousand times more interesting than you would imagine. Let us leave behind the books and films, the scandal and gossip and set out through its streets to meet some of its earlier buildings and their inhabitants.

A visitor to Lucknow in the 1760s would not have found, as is commonly thought, a meagre collection of villages on the banks of the River Gomti, but a large walled medieval town clustered round the Macchi Bhawan fort on the highest land in an otherwise flat, dull plain. The city was already famous for its *bidri* work, silver inlay in gun metal, its textiles and beautiful calligraphy, as well as its tobacco and sugar which were exported as far away as Afghanistan. Walking through the narrow Chowk, which still exists today, the visitor would have passed the Royal Mint striking coins in the name of the Mughal emperor, and the buildings of the Farangi Mahal, a Muslim seminary. But he would have searched in vain for the foreigners who gave their name to the palace now inhabited by the learned *mullahs*.

A hundred years earlier a small community of Britons from the newly formed East India Company had been ordered to export to Bombay the fine cottons made in Lucknow. Houses were built or bought here in the 1640s for the Company officials who complained piteously about their isolation from the great cities of India, but who nevertheless lived in considerable style. The cottons, known as *dereabauds* were washed and processed on the north bank of the Gomti, but difficulties in transporting the goods across Mughal India proved too great and after 30 years or so, the British factory was shut down as being 'too remote' and expensive. The Company houses were later bought by the Emperor Aurangzeb and made over to the clerics, but the name of the foreigners palace still reminds us of Lucknow's first British connection.

At the end of the Chowk stood the Macchi Bhawan fort, a forbidding, wall-encircled collection of inner courtyards, houses, gardens and gateways, high above the banks of the Gomti. It was here, in the mid-18th century that another group of foreigners settled – the Nawabs of Awadh. Only slightly less exotic than the first Company officials, the Nawabs came from Naishapur in Iran, and they brought their own language, manners, clothes and architecture as well as their Shi'ite ceremonies to the Hindu city of Lucknow. Although the Nawabs lived in Lucknow for less than a century they left an ineradicable mark on the city, and during that time it flourished as few Indian cities have done before, attracting the most talented artists, the wittiest writers, the most beautiful courtesans and the most skilled artisans, all drawn to the magnet of the Nawabi Court.

With the vigour of the new immigrant the Nawabs made Awadh into an independent kingdom, but their success soon attracted envious British eyes and this time the Company was more interested in politics than cotton. Even before Asaf-ud-Daula, the fourth Nawab, made Lucknow his capital in 1775, the Company had decided that the new 'royal' family needed a British Resident. His brief was clear: he was to cement 'the friendship between the Company and the Nawab and to obtain large sums of money said to be due from him' – a shameless reason for all subsequent interference in the short-lived kingdom by the Company. We shall walk over the deserted Residency site later, but the most interesting Europeans to be met with in the city at this time were the free-booting adventurers also attracted to the glittering court.

They were giants among men, these early travellers, even at a time when India was attracting the most vigorous and imaginative immigrants, with the promise of untold wealth to be got by anyone who survived the meteorological and political climate. Antoire Polier, a Swiss architect was one such man. Working at first as chief engineer for the Company, he was seduced by the charm of Lucknow and became court architect to Asaf-ud-Daula. Polier also found time to serve both in the Nawab's army and the Company's force, for in those days no one thought it odd to have two or even three completely different but simultaneous careers.

Specialization was considered eccentric, and when not fighting or building, Polier was experimenting as a perfumer, making *attar* or perfume of roses from his Lucknow gardens and collecting Indian miniatures, then almost totally ignored by Europeans. It is sad that this gifted man, who was killed in a duel in Paris in 1794, left so few traces of his time in the city. He almost certainly worked on the *ba'oli*, a water palace cunningly cut into the Macchi Bhawan hill. A flight of steps led down to a tank filled from the waters of the Gomti and around three sides of the tank arose a honeycombed structure of cool, airy rooms, lined with marble and red porphyry and pierced by little balconies.

The ba'oli, now stripped of its finery is all that remains of the Macchi Bhawan fort, for everything above ground was dynamited in 1857 by Sir Henry Lawrence, who judged, quite rightly, that the fort would be impregnable if captured by Indians during the uprising. Only the semi-subterranean water palace escaped destruction, and the Lucknow Medical College now stands on the levelled site above.

But even Polier has been overshadowed by the best known European in Lucknow, the Frenchman Claude Martin. The two contemporaries were, not surprisingly, good friends, sharing the same interests, language and to a large extent the same occupations. Martin too, worked for both the Company and the Nawabs, having first come to Awadh as a surveyor. Though now known only for his buildings in the city, he was primarily an entrepreneur, never hesitating to supply exactly what was needed by anyone, at exactly the right time and for the right price. Whether it was mirrors from Europe for the Nawab, houses to rent for the British Residency staff, guns and ammunition for Indian princes, an unsecured loan, hot-air balloons or military advice, Martin was the man. He trod the delicate tightrope between the Court and the Company without ever losing his footing and died in 1800 regretted by all and a millionaire of his time.

Much of his money came from land. He had bought a large area near the Macchi Bhawan that was to become the Residency and he hired out the first houses to the British staff there. He owned gardens and farms, producing roses and indigo, as well as a riverside bazaar on the Gomti.

Martin's first town house was the Farhad Baksh, east of the Residency which later became part of a Nawabi palace. Our imaginary visitor, now transposed to the 1780s would have found this curious building impossible to enter, except by invitation. Sited on the Gomti it had a deep moat round three sides with a drawbridge facing the city. Cannons which Martin himself had cast were mounted on the roof, providing a strange contrast with the delicate stucco swags and garlands which decorated the upper storeys. Inside, each room could be closed by thick iron doors and anyone besieged there could retreat until they reached the single spiral staircase leading to the roof with its telescope and armoury.

Conversely one could also descend into the lower storeys which were designed to flood each monsoon. As the water level crept down during the spring months, so too did Martin, into his cool underground retreat, the riverside door and windows covered with damp *khus ki tattis* or fragrant grass blinds. Even today, when the Farhad Baksh has become the Central Drug Research Institute, the basement levels remain flooded, for engineers believe any attempt to pump them dry would lead to the collapse of the building.

La Martiniere, Martin's palace-tomb to the southeast of Lucknow exhibited the same fascination with defence and hydraulics. This extraordinary building, much described, was extended in the 1840s and became the school immortalized by Rudyard Kipling in *Kim* as St. Xaviour's. At Martin's death only the central portion was complete. One interior iron door remains today, leading down to his simple basement tomb originally guarded by four life size wooden soldiers. Statuary, was another of Martin's passions. He taught his Indian workforce how to build up figures of brick and plaster round iron skeletons and old photographs of Lucknow show every palace adorned with these most un-Islamic ornaments. Many of the figures which decorate the terraces of La Martiniere today, however, are replacement for those destroyed in the earthquake of 1803 which brought nodding Chinese mandarins and French shepherdesses crashing earthwards in stony confusion.

Martin's last building, barely designed at his death was Barowen, or Musa Bagh, a country palace four miles west of Lucknow. Because none of Martin's plans exist today for his buildings, it is impossible to claim Barowen entirely as his conception, though the skilful use of underground rooms cut into the hill to guard against the summer heat recall the Frenchman's other works. This lovely building, one of the happiest examples of the Indo-European style in Lucknow, rose majestically from the banks of the Gomti.

There were grand reception rooms for the Nawabs and their guests, who approached it by river, and a shady courtyard with underground rooms for the women of the court. The quality of the decoration was so high that even after nearly 200 years, coloured stucco blinds can still be seen over the doorways, neatly imitating rolled-up tattis. Today Barowen decays quietly, disturbed only by villagers who need building material and see a ready quarry there.

Important as these individual palaces are, it was probably the Nawab Saadat Ali Khan who changed the face of medieval Lucknow more than anyone. Brother and successor to Asaf-ud-Daula, the Nawab was one of the great 19th century town planners, though he was seldom given credit for more than dabbling with the new Grecian style of architecture. He carved out the broad street known today as Hazratganj, running from the country house of Dilkusha in the east to the Chattar Manzil palaces near the Residency.

By 1815 our imaginary visitor would not have entered Lucknow through the old Chowk, but along the broad new street where sumptuous processions would pass, the jewelled elephants bearing nawabi guests to the palace past stuccoed European houses shimmering with gold tissues draped over the balconies. Hazratganj itself was barred by a series of gateways spanning the road like bridges, which according to a traveller, were European on one side and Moorish on the other, the term then used for the Lucknow style. It was undoubtedly one of the finest roads in India, leading to the delightful houses of the Nawab, each set in gardens where artificial ponds and canals ran in perfect symmetry and where nightly fireworks and silver trees transformed the scene into an Arabian fairy land.

Yet it was this almost theatrical quality of buildings like the Darshan Bilas and the Chota Chattar Manzil that provoked harsh criticism from European visitors to the city. Architectural writers in particular have never liked Lucknow. Scorn was poured on its hybrid buildings which were condemned for being neither one thing nor the other, neither Indian nor European, and it is tedious to repeat the cries of 'Fake! Sham! Imposter!' which sprang from the lips of those who seldom spent more than a few days in the city. Critics ignored the vitality of the Indo-European style and the Indian gift for rapid assimilation and translation of new ideas into something unique.

If we now set down an English man or woman in these same streets in the late 1830s we would, with amusement, watch them scuttling head down towards the enclave of the British Residency, now grown alarmingly from the first thatched bungalows and

Martin's rented houses. Once through the Baillie Gate entrance the visitor could relax in a small corner of Victorian England, safe from the noise and colour of the exotic city outside.

The days of the liberal 18th century European were over. The new Nawab, Nasir-ud-din Haider had been forced by the Company to sack most of his English staff, though he still maintained an unrequited passion for the West, even marrying two English women who lived in Lucknow. There were no more self-taught architects like Martin and Polier. The Company now 'lent' engineers to the Nawabs to build canals, schools, roads and other sensible buildings. An insularity had fallen over the British community, reflected in the prim Residency houses with their neat lawns, gravelled drives and iron gates.

The Residency itself was a dismal building, adhering to no particular style, and it was only the Banqueting Hall, built by Saadat Ali Khan for the Company which raised the area from the prosaic. Across the lawns sat the small Gothic church, designed deliberately to contrast with the 'towering mosques and gilded temples' of the city, but criticized even by its clergyman for its smallness and fake rose window.

It was the uprising of 1857 which immortalized the Lucknow Residency in British mythology. Rightly, the heroism of its British and Indian defenders during the dreadful six months siege has not been forgotten, though the real story of life inside the Residency has never been tackled, except in a fictionalized account by J.G. Farrell: *The Siege of Krishnapur*. The Residency which had grown up piecemeal since 1775 had never been designed for defence, it was residential. Desperate makeshift barricades were constructed out of anything that came to hand – the Resident's furniture, books, packing cases and bizarrely, a Welsh harp. The defenders died from gunshot wounds, but illness and malnutrition also filled the new graveyard near the church.

It is still a moving experience to read the litany of the dead in the haunted overgrown cemetery, but the sight that brings real tears to the eyes is the desolation of Qaisarbagh, the last palace of the Nawabs. Built in an amazingly short period between 1848 and

1852 by the last Nawab, Wajid Ali Shah, the buildings, standing off Hazratganj are a rebuke to the British who dynamited the area in 1857 and the Indians who let them decay. Today, it is only from a series of photographs taken in March 1858, that one can form any idea of the grandeur, wit and style of this extraordinary complex. Surrounded by double storeyed terraces and pierced by elaborate gateways, the inner gardens held a series of unique buildings which served no other purposes than to please the eye.

There was the Lanka, an ornamental bridge over dry land, with its four domed towers, the double spiral staircase which led nowhere, decorated with plaster women holding hoops, clearly inspired by Martin's earlier statuary. There was, most curious of all, the only classical pigeon house in India, probably in the world, a two storey narrow avian Parthenon, as well as the Mermaid gate with its voluptuous fish-tailed women tempting one further into the heart of the palace. To one side of the great garden stood the grandest building of all, the Roshan-ud-daula Kutcheri, with its 'Ionic columns, balustrades with globe-like finials, Moorish minarets, Hindu umbrellas… all blended in a confusion which the eye may seek vainly to disentangle and surrounded with an unmeaning gilt band', as a confused visitor wrote.

It was the very exuberance of the architecture which took the breath away, the sheer piling up of elements with a creative joy that resulted in a building which in its prime made England's Brighton Pavilion look like a country vicarage. Much less is known about the Qaisarbagh palaces than the earlier Nawabi houses. This is not so strange as it seems, for with increased Company interference in the internal affairs of Awadh, the Nawabs, not surprisingly had become more reticent.

Where 18th century European travellers had been warmly encouraged to visit the Macchi Bhawan and left vivid descriptions of them, by the 1850s Qaisarbagh was described as a mysterious labyrinth into which Wajid Ali Shah would disappear with his strange retinue of female soldiers, known as the Amazons. Only once a year would the palace be open for the *Yoghi* ceremony, when everyone was bidden to wear yellow, and the Nawab, dressed as a *fakir*, would hold court under a mulberry tree near the marble *barahderi*, which still remains. There were rumours of more elaborate play acting when the Nawab would don female clothing and perform strange ceremonies with the ladies of the court.

The truth will probably never be known about the secret games played in Qaisarbagh, but we do know that Wajid Ali Shah was a gifted poet, writing under the pen name, Akhtar, and a sensitive, compassionate man. When abruptly dethroned by the Company in 1856 and forced into exile in Calcutta, one of his chief concerns was the welfare of thousands of palace servants whom he had to leave behind. There are pathetic letters from the nawab insisting that they should receive the pensions to which they were entitled, as well as instructions for the many animals left in the private zoos of Lucknow. Thousands of pigeons were released to circle frantically round the empty palaces, and elephants, tigers, antelopes and camels were sold to other zoos or destroyed.

Two years later Qaisarbagh was looted by British soldiers who recaptured the city after 1857, and troops raced through the empty rooms in an orgy of destruction, smashing jade bowls, mirrors and crystal chandeliers, burning priceless gold tissues and prising the jewels out of the thrones. It was one of the most shameful episodes of British rule in India.

But let us leave our time traveller in Qaisarbagh in 1855, before the fall. It provokes unnecessary grief to move him further forward to witness the destruction of the city during the last 140 years. Just occasionally, especially at dusk, as the crows fly behind the peeling stucco domes to the palm trees in Qaisarbagh's remaining garden, one can still catch a little of the lingering vitality of this once splendid city, old Lucknow.

Behind the purdah

VIJAY KHAN

THE importance of royal women in the history of Avadh has not been fully appreciated. Their importance is made even greater because the *zenana* has always been a world unto itself, impenetrable and inscrutable. Indeed, one is forced to ask that had some of the wives and mothers been the rulers of Avadh instead of their husbands and sons, would the course of history of Avadh been different? It is in fact often forgotten how crucial the role of some of the Begums of Avadh was during this time, not only in response to the changing times and its compulsions, but to the little that has survived today of that great efflorescence of what came to be described by *Avadhi* and *Lucknowi* culture.

Not only did the presence and patronage of Nawab Begum and Bahu Begum safeguard and foster the magnificence of Faizabad, it came to be crucial for the protection and perpetuation of the line of Avadh. It was these two women and later others, who helped steer Avadh through a glorious, even though sad history. It was in the hands of these women, whether Nawab begum or Bahu Begum, Badshah Begum or Malika Kishwar, that its culture found shape and drew sustenance. And even when the crown of Avadh had been finally seized in 1856, it was Hazrat Mahal, one of its begums, who remained intransigent and fought for its restoration.

The steady dereliction of Imperial Delhi in the 18th century gave Avadh the bricks and mortar for its foundation. While the dynasty which grew on this foundation lasted for a 136 years (d. 1722-1856), it knew only in its early years the strength and integrity which comes from true sovereignty. The informal independence gained from the Mughals by Avadh was soon replaced by its dependence on the new imperial force of the day, the British East India Company. Shuja-ud-daula's defeat by the British at the battle of Buxar in 1764 sealed the fate of Avadh and put it into the political grip of the British based in Calcutta. Their hold tightened continually until grip became grab and in 1856 the Avadh dynasty ended.

The political history of Avadh has a quality of sad inevitability. It is strung together by the rule of puppet-like figures, of whom some were more difficult to manipulate than others. A few of the nawabs, even though powerless remained responsible and occasionally even intransigent to British strategy and pressure. Others made not even the pretence of office but grew bleary in the haze of pleasure, in its device and pursuit.

It was perhaps this political stalemate, which had done away with the need for the soldier-statesman such as the first three rulers of Avadh, from which emanated a peculiar calm and security. Such a state of affairs not only stimulated a unique cultural efflorescence, but attracted and produced some unusual men and women.

Avadh, its dynasty, culture and commerce first began in a settlement made by Burhan-ul-Mulk Sa'adat Ali Khan on the banks of the river Ghagra, near a *keora* or screw-pine jungle. This became known as Faizabad and later, in his nephew and successor Safdar Jung's time, as Bangla, after the mud *bangla* or shooting box that Burhan-ul-Mulk had built for himself. Although Shuja-ud-daula, Safdar Jung's son and heir, had chosen Lucknow as his capital, he was persuaded to return to Faizabad after 1761.

Contemporary descriptions of Faizabad are few but vivid. Shuja-ud-daula built and rebuilt its bastions, recruited and organized the army, planned its gates and gardens, its markets and mansions. Very soon, while Faizabad's fame made people think nothing of abandoning Shahjahanabad (Delhi), the lure of profit made the unknown seem a piece of cake for merchants from China, Persia, Europe and Afghanistan. In the streets, gardens and markets of Faizabad, men from far corners of India mingled with those from distant lands. They came again and again, while many stayed on. Shuja-ud-daula had some 200 Frenchmen attached to his court who were employed to train the army and direct the manufacture of arms. Among these was also the well-known Claude Martin. According to a contemporary, Faizabad became a city in which 'no one as much as dreamed of poverty and distress.'

With Shuja-ud-daula's untimely death in 1775, the existence of Faizabad was suddenly threatened. This threat however, came to be cushioned for a few years by the presence of two remarkable women, Shuja-ud-daula's mother, Nawab Begum and his wife, Bahu Begum.

Nawab Aliya Sadrunissa Begum, Nawab Begum and her daughter-in-law, Jenab Aliya Mualiya Amat-uz-Zehra, famous as Bahu Begum, dominated not merely the zenana, but the polity and politics of the early history of Avadh. Indeed for a time it seemed as if two capitals co-existed, Faizabad and Lucknow, one dominated by the will of two women, the other by the whims of its rulers. They lived in the strictest of segregation from men in a zenana where a boy of six was too old to enter.

The segregation of women from men was part of the ethos of the East. Its origins lay in the tenets of Islam but its influence was widespread, especially in India. Segregation or *purdah* (literally curtain), came to partly represent position and wealth in society apart from becoming the means of protecting women from outsiders, strangers and indeed all men other than those of the family. Purdah also became part of the etiquette of modesty in parts of India within the zenana so that younger women in deference covered their faces even in the presence of senior female in-laws.

The begums, therefore, lived among their countless attendant women, defied and resisted, intrigued and ruled, all within the window-less bastions and courtyards of the zenana. Indeed had some of the begums of Avadh been less independently wealthy and less formidable, they may have escaped notice as so many did, whether of British officialdom, of prominent courtiers or of contemporary writers.

The financial independence of these begums lay in the dowries they received at the time of their marriage. Some dowries were legendary in size, while some, a mere pittance. Among the begums of Avadh, Nawab Begum, and even more so her daughter-in-law, Bahu Begum, happened to be extremely rich women in their own right. Nawab Begum was the daughter of the first ruler of Avadh and was married to the second, while her daughter-in-law came from a prominent Persian family whose grandfather was attached to the court of Emperor Aurangzeb in Delhi.

Not only did their dowries consist of invaluable jewellery, gold, silver, clothes, elaborate household effects, horses, elephants, cattle, servants, a token army, but also of villages and indeed entire districts. Legally this was always their property and not that of their husbands. The land provided them with revenue throughout their lives. Apart from this dowry, an appropriate *meher* or dower was fixed at the time of marriage which could be claimed by the wife from her husband at any time. Even though this meher was rarely claimed, it was part of Muslim law and was far from being an empty formality. Moreover, both these women survived Shuja-ud-daula, the son of the one and husband of the other and thus inherited a great deal of his property.

Commensurate to their influence and importance, little is known and even less has been written about these begums. Later there were a few English women who saw behind the purdah of the zenana. They faithfully recorded and reported their impressions to friends and family in England who, with an equal sense of history, collected and compiled these for posterity. While these impressions are quite invaluable for the glimpse they give us into a lifestyle, which even the most unbridled of imaginations may find difficult to recreate, they have distinct limitations. For one thing, they are often compilations of visual impressions, rather than of observations based upon knowledge. Fanny Parkes, Emily Eden, Meer Hassan Ali (an English woman who married a Lucknowi) and many others, may have seen a great deal but they simply did not speak Persian, Urdu or Hindustani well enough to comment upon the conditions and complexity of the lives of women in purdah.

Having to live within a restricted space, however spacious, for all their lives, seemed to have made women the guardians of culture, of its traditions and customs and also of language. It was perhaps for this reason that a simple matter like story-telling became a matchless art during this time. The begums did not share the freedom of their husbands and sons who could make rules as easily as they could bend or break them.

The imperial zenana in Delhi was a vast and complicated part of the Mughal administration. Its pattern was adopted in Avadh. The zenana of the nawab-wazirs of Avadh consisted of a separate building or set of buildings. Its architecture was rather ordinary by comparison to the palaces and residences the nawab-wazirs and later the Kings of Avadh built for themselves. The zenana built by Burhan-ul-Mulk however, was built of mud as his own residence was, a far cry from the zenana of his daughter Sadrunissa and all those who followed.

The basic dictates of the zenana left little room for architectural innovation. Its type remained unaltered even into the early part of this century. The buildings of this royal establishment were large and rectangular whose walls rose to the roof unbroken by any opening on at least three of its sides.

Within the building there was a principal courtyard open to the sky. Framed by wide, covered corridors, these had on their outer edges at regular intervals, handsome pillars which supported the attenuated arches distinct of Avadh architecture. On to these long covered corridors opened the living quarters of the chief begum. It could well be that one room occupied more or less the entire side of this large courtyard, while another consisted of the private *imambara* of the begum, a third of some more rooms and bath chambers and the fourth of an entrance which connected the other parts of the zenana or even the outside world. There were endless other courtyards all connected, surrounded by halls, rooms, offices, stores, dispensaries, kitchens, *aab-khanas* or store-rooms for water, *tosha-khanas* or store-rooms for valuables, and other imambaras.

The beauty and dignity of some of these rooms lay in their simplicity. By comparison to the rooms and halls outside, they were bare and uncluttered. The floors were always covered with a spotless white cloth, *chandni,* and by the time of Ghazi-ud-din Haider (1814-1827) often overhung by Bohemian or Venetian chandeliers. At most there were the traditional low beds used by the poor and rich alike, distinguished not by design as much as by whether the legs were covered by gold or silver or were just of plain wood. Brass and silver lamps, *chiraag-daans,* stood in corners, while by the bedside stood a spittoon, *ugal-daan,* and a large, elaborate betel-nut and betel-leaf box, *paan-daan,* delicately crafted with gold and silver.

And yet not a corner of these rooms, halls and courtyards was ever empty. The mere presence of some of its begums, larger than life, filled these vast spaces with their majesty.

When holding court, the begum sat on a bejewelled seat or *musnad* supported by matching cushions and bolsters, whose pearls and precious stones were held in place by exquisite embroidery in gold and silver thread. Somewhere in the folds of the rich satin, silk, or gold-cloth of her *pyjama,* held at her waist by intertwined bands of gold and silver, off whose tassels tinkled emeralds, pearls and rubies, was a *peshqabz* or dagger, its tip poisoned, its blade incomparable, its hilt bejewelled. The sun played on the rubies and pearls of her large gold *nath,* a nose-ring, a sign of being married as well as that the husband was alive, while her *dupatta* or cloth to cover the head with, of the finest tissue, soft and transparent gleamed like a sheet of dew. This variety of cloth was in fact called *shabnum* or dew. If the begum was a widow, however, she was jewelless, her dress was plain with its colours sombre and subdued. In either circumstance there was a beautiful *ganga-jamuni* box, the gold being compared to the river Ganga, the silver to the Jamuna, containing made up betel-leaf cones beside her, and a *pechican*, a *huqqa* used by women, whose base may have been of perfect crystal, *billur*, or of fine filigree.

The ultimate favour that a begum could bestow upon someone was a betel-leaf cone, a *gilori* or *paan*, from her own *khas-daan* or a puff at her huqqa. And occasionally as an indication of favour and equality, a lady may have been asked to share the begum's musnad. Generally, however, the women sat in front of her on the plain white chandni. The conversation was varied, the voices muffled as they can only be with a paan stuffed into one side of the mouth.

On the other hand, the begum may have been seated in her room dictating or telling her secretary about matters ranging from communications with officials 'outside', to orders related to aspects of zenana administration. Drafts of these orders were made by the appropriate secretary which then had to be approved by the begum before these were signed, sealed and dispatched. It was through written notes that the begum exercised her power and prerogative. Nawab Begum stood out amongst all the begums of Avadh as being a brilliant letter writer and was known to be extremely exacting of her draftsmen. The begum's secretaries and drafts-men could be both men and women. Muhammad Faiz Baksh was one such man, employed at first by Nawab Begum and later by Bahu Begum. He will always be remembered for his valid account of the life and times of both these begums in Faizabad.

When men were in attendance, elaborate arrangements were made to safeguard the privacy of the zenana by curtaining it off from any possible view. The begum would receive him seated behind a heavy curtain. Communication was never direct but conducted with the help of a eunuch or female attendant who also stood behind the curtain. The woman would repeat the message of the man on the other side after having delivered his elaborate messages of respect and homage to the begum even though she could hear him perfectly clear.

The begum would whisper her reply to her secretary, lest her voice be heard, who would repeat this to the man. Not only was it unthinkable that any man so much as see the hem of the begum's dress, it was almost worse, were he to hear the echo of her voice.

And if by some stroke of misfortune the begum felt more than an ordinary headache and a *hakim* or doctor was required, the curtains were more closely drawn than ever. No matter how serious the illness, no more than the hand was offered to the hakim through the curtain, to make his diagnosis by feeling the pulse.

If, after having dealt with matters of state, the begum was tired, she retired to her room. Two women massaged her feet and legs, another two her arms and back, and yet some more fanned her. Usually, at the bottom of the begum's bed sat another woman who attempted to induce sleep in her mistress by her talent of story-telling.

Thus, in attending to the begum, waves of women busied themselves, making the walls resound and the space shrink. Theirs was a hierarchy whose functions were as varied as of soldiers and guards dressed as men – of palanquin bearers, messengers, secretaries and accountants, of cooks with different specialization, of hosts of attendants, each responsible for a different aspect of the begum's personal care and toilet, of story-tellers and scores of general servants.

There were the ubiquitous eunuchs, the *khwaja-saras*. When despotism combined with polygamy, their employment came to be regarded as a compelling necessity to guard women in the Middle and Far East. Indeed eunuchs dominated the zenana hierarchy. Some became powerful and important as confidantes and favourites of their begums. As they had no heirs, the wealth they accumulated during their careers reverted back to the state after their death.

The majestic seclusion of the zenana, however, was no barrier to the threat Nawab Begum, but much more so, Bahu Begum, came to pose to Asaf-ud-daula, the grandson of the one and the son of the other, to his successors and indeed to the British.

Sadrunissa was the oldest daughter of Burhan-ul-Mulk, Subedar of Avadh. She was married to his nephew and successor Mirza Muhammad Muqum better known as Safdar Jung, in around 1724. The bride was about 12 years old while the bridegroom was about 15 or 16 years of age. Whether Sadar-e-Jahan, Sadrunissa or Nawab Begum was beautiful or plain may perhaps never be known, the purdah being so stringent. It is, however, known that Safdar Jung never married again nor ever sought the company of other women, being deeply attached to his wife. For this Safdar Jung must surely be singled out among the other rulers of Avadh, some of whom married as many as 700 times.

Not only was Nawab Begum endowed with qualities of fair play, justice and deep personal piety, she combined unusual political astuteness with commanding courage. If the dynasty of Avadh survived the death of its founder Burhan-ul-Mulk in 1739, it was essentially because of his daughter's wisdom and foresight.

Nadir Shah plundered Delhi the year Burhan-ul-Mulk died. The landlords and small chiefs who had been effectively subdued by Burhan-ul-Mulk, raised their heads and arms again in an attempt to secure their individual independence. In his capacity as the Nawab of Avadh, Safdar Jung was hesitant to face them despite his superior military strength, lest he be defeated. Had it not been for Nawab Begum's forceful prompting which eventually culminated in success, there may have been no further history of Avadh. This was not the only instance when her involvement and insight proved crucial.

Nawab Begum's court and courtiers maintained the peace and pomp of Faizabad. While there is no doubt that the basis of the court style of Avadh was Mughal, it came to acquire a distinction which was unique and Avadhi.

Perhaps the obvious factor lay in the difference of religion, Sunni Delhi, Shia Avadh. In other words, while the stamp of culture of Imperial Delhi was Persian, as indeed was the court language, the Persians themselves were Shia as opposed to their Sunni masters. The Persians were therefore compelled to practice their religion with caution and care, even though they were often the most important officials of the court.

In Avadh this was immediately reversed. The rulers and their court, who were mostly Shia, became the dazzling guardians, and as it were, the direct successors of Shia Safavid Persia. For the underpinning of Avadh culture was Shia faith and practice, centred around the martyrdom of the Prophet's family. Its impetus, development and distinct style must in significant measure be associated with women led by the Begums of Avadh, especially Nawab Begum and Bahu Begum.

As the death of Nawab Begum was sudden in 1796, it caused enormous consternation among the people of Faizabad. There were several important eunuchs and nobles from Delhi. Broken in spirit and bereft of all that they had once known and owned, they had gathered in Faizabad. Here their lives had been relit for a few more years by familiar beacons of glory and grandeur. For Nawab Begum's style had been in keeping with that of the late Mughals, the Emperors Aurangzeb and Bahadur Shah I. The peoples' livelihood, peace and prosperity had emanated from her presence and bounty.

With her death, Nawab Begum's establishment broke up and scattered. Had it not been for Bahu Begum, apart from the fall of Nawab Begum's establishment the whole city of Faizabad would have collapsed. Instead, Faizabad flourished for yet a few more years under the aegis of Bahu Begum, the splendour of whose court outshone even that of the dead begum.

Amat-uz-Zehra, later famous as Jenab Aliya Muta'aliya Bahu or daughter-in-law, Bahu Begum was probably born in 1729. Originally from Persia, her grandfather had achieved considerable prominence at the court of Emperor Aurangzeb in Delhi, as the chief superintendent of the royal household. In 1745 or thereabout, Amat-uz-Zehra was married to Jalal-ud-din-Haider, better known as Shuja-ud-daula. It appears however, that this marriage only took place at Emperor Muhammed Shah's behest as Shuja-ud-daula was most reluctant. No marriage had cost as much as this one, not even the marriage of

Emperor Shah Jahan's son Dara Shikoh. The marriage cost 46,00,000 rupees as against the 32,00,000 spent for Dara Shikoh's wedding.

Bahu Begum's wealth was enormous and became of great consequence. It was crucial to her husband and came to draw much attention throughout her life; from those nearest to her son Nawab-Wazir Asaf-ud-daula, to those farthest away from her, like the Governor General of Bengal, Warren Hastings.

At first Bahu Begum's wealth was propitious for Avadh, later it tantalized the British Company based in Calcutta. Historians have in fact often questioned the legitimacy of Bahu Begum's wealth, especially in view of the fact that at the time of her husband's death his entire treasury had been entrusted to her by him. They have since argued that by Muslim Shia law of inheritance, only a fraction of this wealth was rightfully hers. While this is true, it must not be forgotten that Bahu Begum was independently very rich and that she demonstrated this independence by several gestures even during the lifetime of her husband.

It was her dowry, larger almost than legend, which more or less bought back Shuja-ud-daula's throne, after his defeat by the British at Buxar in 1764. The British had assessed that Shuja-ud-daula owed to the East Indian Company as a present, four million rupees for his remaining territories which he would have had to otherwise also cede to them. His own treasury being quite empty, Bahu Begum handed over to him her money, gold and jewellery. This, along with the two million rupees given to him by his mother, Nawab Begum, cleared the debt within a few months. It was perhaps this gesture more than anything else which brought the magnanimity and concern of his wife to Shuja-ud-daula's notice. After this he seems to have decided to entrust his finances to Bahu Begum.

The fact that Mirza Amani, famous as Asaf-ud-daula, was the oldest of Shuja-ud-daula's sons by Bahu Begum, was not enough to ensure his succession to the throne of Avadh. Stories regaling his antics and indulgences had begun to circulate in Avadh and even reached the ears of those in Calcutta, while he was still young. Sa'adat Ali, a step-brother was deemed far more suitable by all concerned except by the real power behind the throne, Bahu Begum. She was clearly aware of her son's shortcomings but wanted, more than anything else, to see her own son as successor to her husband. Even Nawab Begum attempted to persuade Bahu Begum from installing Asaf-ud-daula on the throne for she had judged his temperament and recognized its proclivities. Bahu Begum, however, had her way and Asaf-ud-daula became Nawab-Wazir of Avadh. Asaf-ud-daula's accession to the throne of Avadh was to have far reaching repercussions, affecting Bahu Begum herself, the future of Faizabad and ultimately the history of Avadh.

While Bahu Begum was still in mourning for her husband, Asaf-ud-daula approached his mother for six lakh rupees. This was the first of such demands which continued more or less month after month, until in late 1775 he was made to sign a deed renouncing all further claims on his mother's property. This guarantee was attested to by the British Resident, Bristow, on behalf of the Company. The undertaking, however, seemed not to deter Asaf-ud-daula. In 1781, he approached his mother again for what he described as his rightful inheritance. In order to procure this amount Asaf-ud-daula solicited the help of the British. This may have seemed almost too good to be true, for Hastings and the Company were like the Nawab-Wazir in terrible financial straits. Having implicated both the Begums in a conjectured plot of rebellion planned by Raja Chait Singh of Banaras, Hastings decided that Bahu Begum no longer deserved the protection and mediation of the Company as agreed to in the guarantee of 1775.

In 1781 both the Begums were arrested by the British. Jawahir Ali and Bahar Ali, eunuchs, whose position at the court of Bahu Begum was unrivalled, were tortured until they handed over the treasure. Members of the royal zenana and *khurd-mahal* were harassed, humiliated and made to suffer enormous privation.

All this proved to much for even the British in England. On his return to London, Warren Hastings had to face an impeachment trial which lasted from 1788 to 1794. 'The spoilation of the Begum' formed the second charge brought against Hastings, his action having been deemed by the prosecution as 'highly criminal'. It was at this trial that the indictment of Warren Hastings by Edmund Burke and James Mill became famous.

Bahu Begum lost her only son Asaf-ud-daula in 1798. Contrary to the common belief that there was no love lost between mother and son, she was bereft. Since no one could live up to Bahu Begum's style, nor match her stature, this always created much resentment and jealousy in the family. This found expression in the rudeness and indignity they tried to subject her to. Bahu Begum's principal concern, therefore, became her own court in Faizabad, its courtiers, women and servants. She, like Nawab Begum, extraordinarily enough, always had a concern for the lesser wives and women of the khurd-mahal too. She knew that all these people would be left without any shred of succour and redress after her death.

Bahu Begum, therefore, made a will in which she made the East India Company the trustee of her entire property valued at seven million rupees. She did not trust her family. She stipulated that the interest be used as pensions known as *Amanat Wasiqas* for all those named by her in perpetuity. Bahu Begum thus created the first of the wasiqas, a charitable trust peculiar to Avadh and paid only in Lucknow and Faizabad.

Bahu Begum had outlived five rulers of Avadh and had seen the installation of the sixth. She died in 1815, at the age of about 86 and with her died Faizabad.

It is not possible to judge Bahu Begum by ordinary standards. She stood out amongst all, as a woman not merely privileged by birth, marriage and enormous wealth, but because of her intelligence, magnanimity and strength of purpose. Unlike Nawab Begum, Bahu Begum remained illiterate all her life. This never seemed to hamper her perspicacity or tenacity in dealing with the outside world. Like her mother-in-law she always militated against the growing influence of the British. She was quick to see through the British plans of making Avadh a buffer state between themselves in Bengal and the strong Marathas. And yet, when she saw there was no one worthy in her own family, she made the British the trustees of her property after her death.

During her lifetime there were few women and men who could rival her strength or match her dignity in northern India. At the peak of her glory it is said that she had at her command 10,000 troops, an excellent cavalry, innumerable horses and elephants. There were a hundred thousand people whose daily bread depended upon her. Indeed in the words of a contemporary resident of Faizabad: '...all felt as happy and secure as though they were in a mother's arms.'

The city that Burhan-ul-Mulk had founded, that Shuja-ud-daula had adorned and that Nawab Begum had maintained and cherished, became resplendent in the shadow of Bahu Begum. In the history of Avadh, the life and times of Bahu Begum forms a unique, albeit complicated chapter.

Nawabs and kebabs

HOLLY SHAFFER

'*Guth-ti*,' Suleiman Mahmudabad noted, referring to the first liquid to pass a newborn's lips, 'depends on the mother and the father's humours, and the family's characteristics.' We are in conversation in his office, a spare high-ceilinged room except for the enormous desk scattered with books behind which are shelves of more books. Appropriately, his family's very own apothecary where such tea was brewed, had been situated across the corridor.

'The proper herbs were pounded, boiled, liquefied, strained and given to the child by the *hakim*. This was the first thing given, even before mother's milk; it purged the child.'

'That,' he said, 'is the beginning of cuisine.'

Meaning the cuisine of Lucknow, where food is not just about food, as in taste, but also context. Lucknow is the city of 'Nawabs and Kebabs' as it was first coined to me, the city of royal extravagance and vibrant street life; of the aristocrat's intricate and playful haute cuisine, and the affordable yet equally satisfying street food and how the two intertwine, particularly through the rituals of Shi'ism. The city where food is spiced specific to the person through the hakim, or doctor of Yunani medicine; where food is dependent on the etiquette and manners of serving, with Urdu sweetly on the lips. The city where a tough bit of meat is ridiculed, and nearly every dish made richer with cream, more fragrant with *keora* water, and more tender through slow *ghee*-infused cooking. As Abdul Halim Sharar so elegantly puts forth in the 1880s, in his story-brimming catalogue of its rarified culture, or *tehzeeb*, 'Lucknow's diet is the most salient guide to its refinement.'[1]

Historical Nawabi cuisine is found today in traces, through cobbling together sources: 19th century cookery books, travel diaries, and paintings, as well as histories and stories of the personages of the city; the descendants of the Nawabs, or noblemen to the Mughals who governed Lucknow between 1753-1856, and patronized an efflorescence of the arts as the British usurped their sovereignty; descendents to the taluqdars and zamindars,[2] the large and small rural landholders of Awadh who became the ruling elite at the behest of the British after the Mutiny or the First War of Independence, 1857; caterers found in *bawarchitola*, or cook's area; and specialized cooks of one or two kebabs, or breads, or rich meat gravies that abound in the network of *gullies* in old Lucknow.

It is a matter of cobbling also, because food is never as it was even from yesterday to today. Food is about sustenance, we *need* it, but it is also the trickiest of arts because it is perishable in nature – it is not recordable, and a recipe does not suffice. Food fluctuates with the ingredients themselves, the climate, the cook, the cook's mood, the eater, the eater's mood, the atmosphere.

For instance, I had been wandering in the old city, or Chowk, on the Gol Darwaza side where Raja Thandai is. He offers a milk drink aptly called *thandai* infused with saffron, *khus* syrup (the cool grass like scent, syruped), or *bhang*, which underscores the reason why a blue poison blooded Shiva Shankar sits auspiciously at the back.

---

1. Abdul Halim Sharar, 'The Last Phase of an Oriental Culture' in *The Lucknow Omnibus*, 2001, p. 155.

2. I will refer to both taluqdars and zamindars as taluqdars only.

Raj Kumar Tripathi of Raja Thandai who I had been talking to about cuisine, turned me around and brought me back through the gate, where men sit curled in the roundels at the top surveying the scene, to turn down a small lane to the *jalebi* shop, which stands next to a grassy courtyard.

On our way out, laden with syrupy hot sweets and saffron milk, he gestured to the carved balconies above the shops, and then 'over there' where *'chaval gully'* apparently was. 'This is a place one should not go,' he warned, 'but then...' and he indeed grew misty-eyed, 'during *shaam-i-Awadh*' meaning the twilight of Lucknow, indicating the charming evening hours between sunset and night, when the air cools, and people of all kinds and types wander the streets for food and entertainment.

Chaval gully means lane of rice. Supposedly, the treasure that is pale fragrant rice has no allusion to the women it houses. When I met Mushtaq Naqvi, the Lakhnavi historian later that week, I asked him about this area, and it was he who explained the *tawai'fs,* or courtesans, and their relationship to food. 'You have touched upon a very delicate subject,' he said, with his eyebrows lifted and mouth poised.

'My brother took me; those were the last of their days (1947-48). I was nine or ten. A woman met us in spotless white dress. I thought she was a fairy. She welcomed me with a deep *salaam* and asked, 'May I bring you a cup of tea, or some *sherbet*, my prince?' I stammered because I had to beg for such things at home. She presented it in a very beautiful cup with the perfect mix of tea, sugar and milk smelling of flowers. 'You see,' he continued, with the reverie still bright on his face, 'they served this Nawabi food you ask on. It was the same, but when you go to a tawai'fs place whatever they served, as simple as a *paan*, or a cigarette, they served so nicely, in such a courtly manner that you felt so elevated that you never felt hunger for the food but hunger for the manners.'

Behind the manners, the intimate teaching of the hakim, and the meandering atmosphere of the old city, what were the actual dishes of the Nawabs or later the taluqdars of Awadh? What lay on their *das-tarkhwan*, a crisp white cloth laden sometimes with 70 *pullaos*, and numerous small dishes to be filled, taken away and re-introduced, with service timed as invisible, as one nibbled from this or that, choosing one's fancy? In an haute cuisine that sometimes seems bored of food itself, what regaled its delight?

There were dishes displaying beauty, wealth and subtlety such as the *Moti Pullao* where the silver and gold leaf are mixed with rawa and stuffed into the neck of the chicken, then wound with string. Before serving they are released as baubles so that the pullao shimmers with 'pearls'. Or *Ananas ki Paratha*, each of the 24 layers crisply, lightly defined with an ethereal sweetness, a hint of pineapple.

Or of exoticism and uniqueness such as a *roghan josh* called *Aloo ki Bukhara,* meaning small dried Bukharan plums, never seen in the dish, just flavouring the sauce, and further beautified by the rare colouring of a flower. Or *Uzbeki Gosht*, a delicate *salan* one must step into the Qidwai house to obtain, or *Laab-i-Mashooq*, Mahmudabad's, meaning lips of the beloved, a cake so light it disappears as sweetly as a kiss upon the mouth.

Then there were the dishes that showed hunger for trickery and game-playing: the luscious story of the last Nawab crowned King of Awadh, Wajid Ali Shah inviting Prince Mirza Asman Qadar to dine, and delighting when the Delhi connoisseur purposely mistook a savoury *quorma* for a sweet conserve. And the reciprocal revenge where the poor king tapped into the 51 dishes laid before him to find, one by one, that they were all made of spun sugar.[3]

Or the drama of a *puri* breaking and not birds flying out, which yes was deemed an ordinary affair by the Lakhnavi Urdu short-story writer, Nainer Masood, but rather a monkey, who satiated by opium, sat dozing in the deflating bread. Or a meal where everything was white – from bread to salads to pullao to dessert; the layout white, the silver plates reflecting white and all on a full moon night.

3.   Abdul Halim Sharar, 'The Last Phase of an Oriental Culture', op. cit., p. 157.

Desire for riddle dishes: a *lookmi*, which was in the shape of an egg, the outside made of *rawa*, and when cut in half, the inside, stuffed with *qeema*, minced meat that was shaped as a yolk and painted with saffron and baked. The 'egg', beautiful in shape and appearance, looked hard but when put into the mouth melted.

With such a rarefied, even excessively baroque cuisine, one has to wonder as to its origins, as well as to its relations to the people, a closer relationship than appears at first in a cuisine that seems defined by money spent (Rs 60,000 a month in the kitchen of Asaf-ud-Daula, one of six in his household, an enormous sum[4]), competition, and the unexpected – gastronomy seems to fit perfectly into the culture of Lucknow, and the list of its leisure: animal combats, pigeon flying, kite flying, story telling, music, dance, drama, poetry in forms both weighty and light, headwear, footwear.

As so many scholars write, Awadh as a region and thus Lucknow as its capital, was in a curious position of essential imprisonment as the British slowly took over the Nawab's armed forces and other 'sovereign duties',[5] and their energies turned inwards, towards their city, Lucknow, and onto the arts, inherited from the Mughals, but flowering to a degree of sophistication teetering on the edge of a 'too much'. The saying goes that 'the elegant manners of Lucknow are such that even *rasgullas* are peeled before they are eaten'; refining something that it is barely impossible to refine more.[6] Luring poets and artists from a declining Delhi, and offering new inspiration, in particular with the addition of acute expressional devotion to Shi'ism, Lakhnavi culture sang its loss into beauty, sometimes grave, sometimes exuberantly flippant.

This expenditure included the arts of gastronomy, inherited from the Mughal court (itself a mix of the Turkish/Central Asian/Persian/North Indo-Pakistan), the declining Safavid Court in Iran, from where

4.   Sharar, p. 155.

5.   P.C. Mookherji, *Pictorial Lucknow*, 1883, p. 42.

6.   Veena Talwar Oldenburg. 'The Making of Colonial Lucknow', in *The Lucknow: Omnibus*, 2001, p. 17.

the first Nawab of Awadh, Saadat Ali Khan, emigrated from, and the European (French, English, Portuguese), but refining itself further on its own demands.

In a comparison to Mughlai food, its greatest influence, Lakhnavi food has less spice (due to the Persian influence); smoother textures (supposedly Nawab Asaf-ud-Daula had actually lost his teeth, filling his mouth with a small ball of velvet[7] – but there was an equal attitude that considered chewing boorish); multiple strainings (from the French influence); distinct attention paid to aromas and colours (such as keora and rose water; or feeding animals on specific diets, like saffron pills to infuse their flesh, or gaming for Siberian cranes who feast on saffron during migration); a theory of spices that included arrangements with the hakim and ground spices for taste and whole ones, wrapped up in an easily removed bouquet so as not to offend the palate, for aroma; and a predilection towards richness: the generous use of ghee, cream and nuts, besides dish after dish of meat.

The cuisine of Lucknow at the time of the Nawabs is therefore very much a cuisine of fusion, and it becomes even more richly original when the taluqdars move into the city from their landed regional estates. There is another aspect as well, that of Islam and specifically Shi'ism.

For instance, the origin story of *dum pukht*, the method of cooking made common parlance by the namesake restaurant of the ITC Maurya hotel. Its founding chef, the legendary Imtiaz Qureshi, is from Lucknow's *bawarchitola*, or cook's area of the old city, and his family is historically employed by the Mahmudabad taluqdars.

Though perhaps a meeting of history and marketing brilliance, the menu at Dum Pukht relays the following story: 'With the dual purpose of providing work (meaning food) and beautification of the city, Nawab Asaf-ud-Daula commenced the building of the Bara Imambara during the great famine circa 1780. Labourers worked during the day, and those of higher classes during the night, so their shame

---

7.   Muhamad Umar, *Muslim Society in Northern India*, 1998, p. 403.

was shrouded. According to the menu at Dum Pukht: 'By royal decree, too, arrangements were made to provide food. Enormous containers were filled with rice, meat, vegetables, spices and sealed. Hot charcoal was placed on top and fires lit underneath while slow cooking ensured that food was available day and night. The result was extraordinary, for when the vessels were unsealed, the splendid aromas attracted royal attention and dum pukht as a Nawabi cuisine was born.'

Dum cooking is not native to Lucknow, it is a Persian technique, meaning to slow bake (*dum* means to breathe and *pukht* to cook, dum pukht thus meaning to cut the breath or steam off). The Ain-i-Akbari notes it among the 10 types of spiced meat dishes, the third type of cookery basic to the Mughal courts along with food without meat, and meat with rice. However, what is decidedly unique about Lucknow is the intimate connection between the aristocracy, the foods that were 'gifted' away under religious auspice known as *tabaruk* (blessed food, similar to *prasad* but not a literal transference of blessing) and the foods of the bazaar.

This is the case with the *shir mal,* also found in the gullies of the old city. Sharar writes: 'In Lucknow, Mahumdu [a bread cook] made great improvements on the *baqar khani* [a type of bread] by producing the shir mal which in taste, scent, lightness and delicacy was very much better.' Mahumdu, at its invention, dashed to the nawab, who tore off a small bite, which is immortalized in the shape of the round shir mal lacking a half-moon bite, signifying Nawabi approval.

Sharar continues, 'In a very short time the shir mal gained such popularity in Lucknow that any celebration at which it was not served could not be considered perfect... [it] so increased the esteem in which Mahumdu was held that on the occasion of royal *majlises* and celebrations he sometimes received orders for a hundred thousand shir mals.'[8]

The shir mal, because of its nature as an easily mass-produced bread that keeps, travels well, can be used to roll up kebabs, and

8.   Sharar, 161-2.

is both a luxury item (of the Nawabs) as well as an economically feasible one (because it is bread after all!) was handed out as tabaruk specifically during Muhurrum, the mourning period for Shias – in fact we see paintings and references to shir mals being handed out from atop the elephant that ends the procession during Muhurrum.[9] This does not mean that either the method of cooking or the bread is religious in nature; simply that certain aspects of Shi'ism in Lucknow allowed for the distribution and popularity of certain items. The shir mal, like dum pukht, also indicates that a food of the street can enter into the kitchen of the palace – that chefs, themselves divided into specific trades or specialists in dishes, cooking for large or small numbers, were richly rewarded for their inventions.

Juan Cole and C.A. Bayly have argued that the massive distribution of food on religious occasions was an integral part of the 'late Islamic kingship'[10] economy. The king's expenditure on luxury needs created markets and employment; the construction of huge religious buildings, such as Lucknow's magnificent Imambaras, tombs, mosques and palaces, provided work for grain, and to relieve famines; and festivals, multiplying during the Nawabi period, were occasions for mass public feedings as well as ritual display. Indeed one of the things that makes Lakhnavi cuisine fascinating are the connections between the decadent cuisine of the court and noble families, and the ordinary people and shops of the bazaars. The fact stands that the most famous items from Lucknow, like the *Tunday* and *Kakori kebabs*, shir mal, *nihari*, dum pukht, pullao (more common than *biriyani* as it is deemed more refined), grace both elite and common tables.

You can, in fact, map the above dishes onto the streets of the old city, much how Francois Bernier describes the bazaar of Delhi in the 1660s: the bakers, the nihari makers, the roasted meat sellers[11] etc. For instance, on the Akbari Gate side of the old city there is Rahim's

---

9. Mrs. Mir Ali Hussein, *Observations*, 1832, p. 87; and Mildred Archer, *Company Paintings*, 1955.

10. C.A. Bayly, *Rulers, Townsmen and Bazaars*, 1983, p. 276.

11. Francois Bernier, *Travels in the Mogul Empire*, 1891. Reprint, Asian Educational Service, 2004, p. 250; and Umar, p. 32.

for nihari, the rich meat broth cooked overnight, strained multiple times and flavoured by a spice bouquet. Labourers traditionally eat this in the morning to sustain them through the day. But the Nawabs equally ate it for breakfast, when they had no visitors, so that no one could bear witness to their indulgence in a common food.

To the left of Rahim's is shir mal gully, where Mahumdu's successor's shop of Ali Hussein still stands. And to the right down a street and to the left is the famous Tunday Kebab, his small meat patties crispy on the outside, smooth and spiced on the inside. The kebab boasts 80 spices, but only 30 for taste, the other 50 are prescribed by the hakim – so it digests well. If you continue down this road that cuts a clean slice through the old city, likely an intervention by the British after 1857 to make the myriad incomprehensible streets and gullies more 'legible' for troops and governance,[12] you are back at Raja Thandai.

There is an equally interesting relationship in the post-1857 influence of the taluqdars, who brought the local cuisine of their regional forts, the *qasbahs*, to meld with the cuisine of Lucknow. For instance, a Kakori kebab is meat tenderized to the feathery lightness of whipped cream, just solid enough not to drop off the skewer. A nobleman of Kakori's chefs spent weeks toiling on this invention after a British official declared a kebab at his mango party 'too tough'. Now known as the Kakori kebab, it traces an older lineage to the *dargah*, or saint's tomb in Kakori, where visitors are given this kebab plus *rotis,* as tabaruk or blessed food. The nobleman's kebab was likely an innovation on this food of more humble origin, but with the move of the taluqdars, the Kakori kebab left the context of blessed food at a saint's tomb, and entered the haute cuisine of Lucknow.

Many taluqdars trace their regional roots back farther than the Nawabs, and felt greater allegiance to the Mughals, perhaps because the Nawabs did not entertain them in dialogue for political reasons. Thus 'the landholders made courts of their own, centred on themselves

---

12.   Veena Talwar Oldenburg, 'The Making of Colonial Lucknow', op. cit., chapter two.

and drawing on both the cultural patterns of the Mughal and Awadh courts and also upon local forms.'[13] This is similar to the Kayasths in Lucknow proper, the Hindu scribes and accountants to the Nawabi rulers, who mixed the Nawabi with their own cuisine, which included more vegetables, less meat, and different spicing. Again, their cuisine is a mixture of the court and the local, which yields surprising fresh tastes.

In Barabunki, a series of small townships and landed estates close to Lucknow, meat is not always available, and the produce changes with the seasons, so a speciality in winter might be *rakchochi*, a *chana daal* pasted onto leaves, rolled, and fried, which is common in villages throughout the UP. Or *saag gosht*, which Fatima Rizvi, the bright eyed scholar on Urdu women's literature, explains 'would be made only with spinach [the most refined green] in Lucknow, but in Barabunki there are different greens from the garden we just throw in.' Another differentiation is with ingredients. In Lucknow there are exotic condiments and produce. 'In Barabunki you will have *mashk gosht – mashk kaliya – mashk ka salan...* because that is what is available.' It is frequently this seasonal aspect of food, or regional availability – *besan roti* with garlic chutney in winters, or *numush*, the whipped cream with a layer of dew that is celebrated and awaited – whose roots are in the countryside.

Fatima continues on another thought, 'The whole qasbah might prepare a single dish, though each will be prepared a little differently not just 5-6 miles down the road, but next door.'

There is a dilemma in saying what exactly Lakhnavi cuisine is, even it if is limited to the specific cuisine of the Nawabs. Be it reading numerous glorifying anecdotes in memoirs or novels from the time, perusing recipes or speaking with people who perhaps remember tasting the dish at age eight, or conversing with a chef who is in a lineage going back five or six generations – even then you cannot say that the dish is as it was, because invariably it was different next door. Because of what was there are questions as to whether the Lakhnavi

---

13.   Michael Fischer, *A Clash of Cultures*, 1987, pp. 225-6.

cuisine that *was* still *is,* even if there are food festivals, restaurants and shops that sell its name.

Suleiman Mahmudabad, with a drawn forehead, because he is musing on the slippery *was*, the *was* that in Lucknow is almost a culture in itself, mentions that, 'Attempts can be made to preserve skills, tastes, recipes, but people can invent anything from a name. We have to recognize that the time has passed. It will never be the same, it cannot be the same, for there is a context.'

There has been loss. Not only loss of the recipe but loss of the context. The Mutiny, Partition, changes in patronage, time itself – these events have shifted Lucknow so it only resembles Lucknow. No reason to mourn, time changes. But there is something to be prized in the continuation of tradition (if it's given room to grow), which is still seen in the old city, in the attempts by families to remember ferociously and to make something living again. Still there is an overwhelming sense of *was*. It makes me wonder whether there ever was an *is*. Then you come across a memory.

Suleiman continues, evincing the struggle to cobble together the remnants of a culture: 'There is one thing we are trying to recreate,' and he pauses, delighted. 'A whole bitter gourd, an *achar* or *murabba* made of that. I had it in my childhood. The wonderful thing was that the bitter gourd is extremely bitter, and in this dish the bitterness could not be tasted. The second amazing thing was it looked as if it were a fresh bitter gourd, completely green, but it was filled with nuts, garlic and chillies, and it was sweet and salty. We have tried, but it has gone.'

Handcrafting a culture

LAILA TYABJI

LUCKNOW, like much of India, is full of paradoxes – down-at-heel elegance, raffish charm, indolent culture, *tehzeeb* and thuggery. A city created by male chauvinist nawabs ruled today by a Dalit woman chief minister.

In 1858 William Russell marvelled at its 'vision of palaces, *minars*, domes of azure and gold, cupolas, colonnades and long facades of fair perspective.' He wondered, as he admired 'this fairy tale city' whether it could really be 'the capital of a semi-barbarous race, erected by a corrupt, effete and degraded dynasty.' Dazzled though he was by 'the towers and spires of gold gleaming and glittering in the sun, the turrets and gilded spheres shining like constellations,' he could not help noticing that 'when viewed in detail the gorgeousness of the picture is obscured by a more than ordinary degree of dirt, filth and squalid poverty which are placed in juxtaposition with its grandest features.'

Over a century and a half later, Lucknow is not so very different. Present day visitors share the same enchantment and exasperation.

The dirt and the grandeur, shopkeepers who greet you with a pun and a scented *paan* while shamelessly diddling you over prices, errant scooterists who overtake on the wrong side and then apologize charmingly with a rhyming stanza to the beauty of your eyes, are all part of that extraordinary culture. A culture both material and metaphysical – of food and flower garlands, perfumes and poetry – harking back to a time where conversation was refined to a fine art and a master of humorous *Phabti* monologues or *ghazals* was honoured with a court title. In Lucknow, culture, not just aesthetic and the arts, even the essentials of life were carried to elaborate extremes. The Lucknavi *paratha* of unleavened bread had 18 layers, and each *paincha* of the Lucknow *gharara* divided skirt was made of 12 metres of cloth! Hand craft was at the very centre of this amazing society. The skills and skilful hands still remain; the products somewhat diminished and down-at-heel, as is Lucknow itself.

The hub of Lucknow and its crafts is still the Chowk – the crossroads and central square in the heart of the city where silversmiths, saree vendors, *chikan* embroiderers and gold *zari* sequin workers carry on their business side by side in narrow shops. Slipping off your shoes and sitting cross-legged on pristine white sheets against white bolsters, you can slip backwards into time and get a flavour of the old Lucknow – before jerry-built bungalows replaced the gracious *havelis*, and criminal politicians took the place of exquisitely erudite nawabs.

At Asghar Ali's, the famous perfumers, you can sniff the distilled essence of 200-year-old rose, jasmine, *hina* or *khus*; buy scented betel nut, or drown in the intoxicating fumes of burning sandalwood. Down side streets you can get your saree or *kurta* stamped to your own design for embroidery, or get a scarf worked with the tiny silver wire spangles of *badla mukesh*. *Kabab wallahs* and restaurants selling *nihari* (tongue) and *paya* (trotters) in a succulent, spicy stew vie with the sweet shop *halwais* stirring up spiralling, hot *jalebis, sohan halwa, balushahi* or *balai* in enormous cauldrons.

Food is not just craft; it is a fine art. According to tradition it was the building of the Bara Imambara (a massive complex of shrines, prayer halls and tombs commissioned by Asaf-ud-Daulah in the late

18th century to give employment at a time of economic hardship) that led to the invention of Lucknavi *dum* or 'pressure' cooking. The cooks hired by the nawab to feed the labourers devised this method of slow, steam cooking so that relays of hungry men could get hot, fresh food through the night. The *kakori* and *galauti* kababs, fish and *biryani* rice of Lucknow are still famous. And as for that curliqued and convoluted Imambara plasterwork – like most of Lucknow, there's more in it than meets the eye! The Rumi Darwaza, that great, equally over-decorated, apparently purely ornamental, arched doorway of brick and coloured stucco, withstood the British nine-pound cannon-shot for over an hour's bombardment, proving indestructible.

Back to the Chowk and the muffled hammering of workers in the narrow side lanes beating silver into paper-thin *warak* silver-leaf for sweetmeats and paans, a counterpoint to the raucous cries of street vendors, and the more politely phrased invitations of the Chowk's famed chikan embroidery traders to enter and view their produce.

Chikan embroidery is another of Lucknow's paradoxes. Tucked into the dingier corners of its elaborately curliqued stucco-work palaces and arched gateways are narrow, winding, over-populated lanes and dark, squat houses inhabited by women who are themselves enveloped in gloomy, black *burkha* veils and desperately poor, oppressed not just by economics but by their own social and domestic circumstance. Illiterate, devoutly Muslim, locked into marriages and family structures that allow little room for individual expression or creativity, they produce one of the most subtle and sensitive of India's myriad embroidery traditions. The delicate, pristine white-on-white shadow and shade of *chikankari*, the epitome of fastidious refinement and esoteric elegance emerging from these dim, dirty, tenement dwellings – children, chickens and goats squabbling, squealing and defecating in each corner, cooking pots smoking – is one of the miracles and mysteries of this fairly complex city.

How chikan originated, even what its name means is, appropriately enough, an equal mystery. There are those who would have it – like everything else in the universe from space satellites and

Jesus Christ to the more obscure sexual acrobatics – that it was all written down in the Vedas. D.N. Saraf in his book on *Indian Crafts* cites travellers to the court of Harshavardhana of Kannauj referring to delicate muslin draperies embellished with motifs worn by the royal harem. But these could have as well been woven as embroidered.

Folklore and one's wilder jingoist fantasies apart, historical research, supported by the ancestral memories of master craftsmen, seems to suggest that chikankari stems from the white-on-white embroidery of Shiraz and came to India as part of the cultural baggage of the Persian nobles at the Mughal court, along with *kalamkari* textile painting, silk carpets, blue tile work and *pietra dura*. Twelfth century Persian poets were already using the word chikan as a metaphor for needle. Though *Shirazi* embroidery is done on coarse, unbleached linen, its repertoire of pulled, drawn thread, knotted, chain and overlaid stitches is strikingly similar to those in the chikankari tradition. Legend has it that it was Empress Noor Jehan, a noted aesthete and embroiderer, who, while making an Eid cap for her husband, the Emperor Jehangir, conceived the idea of using the fine white cotton mull for which Indian weavers were famous, as a base for her stitchery.

Be that as it may, it is well authenticated that the Mughal court adored and patronized chikan embroidery and gave it its own distinctive character and design identity. Chikan was used for everything – from turbans and veils to *angrakhas*, *chogas* and palace interiors. The imperial Mughal manuscript copy of the *Padshahnama* (exhibited some years ago at the National Museum) has a beautiful detail of a many-arched balcony curtained with flowing, sheer white-on-white draperies with delicate floral motifs, which could well be chikan. The cool understated refinement of chikan suited the sophisticated elegance of the Mughals, just as it did the searing heat of an Indian summer. The floral *jaals*, rosettes and paisleys that remain a part of the chikan tradition today are a legacy of their style and imagery – unchanged though occasionally distorted through the years.

Chikan, as Bernier, the 16th century French doctor and traveller reminds us, is ephemeral. He had a keen eye for the finer details of both Indian women and Indian textiles. He described the court ladies drawers, 'enriched with fine needle embroidery, ... so fine and delicate that ... they last only one night, even though they are often worth ten or twelve crowns...' The under-drawers and over-gowns are gone but their stylized, exquisite motifs have come down to us: preserved through the wooden printing blocks with which chikan motifs are transferred onto cloth for embroidery. Converted today into 20th century three-dimension by the labouring hands of women, working in situations and surroundings not much changed from their 16th century sisters.

The lanes around the Lucknow central Chowk still echo to the *thhup-thhup* rhythm of thousands and thousands of kurtas and sarees being printed. Traditionally they were printed in washable terracotta *geru* colour. Today they use the laundry man's Robin Blue! Brokers, all men, generally exploitative male chauvinists, carry the work back to the *bastis* to be embroidered. Working on piece wages, the embroidery women do not themselves engage in outside commercial transactions.

A striking exception is SEWA Lucknow, begun by two young social workers in the mid-1980s. Working in the Lucknow urban slums, they were horrified to discover the miserable pittance the women got for long hours of blinding work. Its imperial origins long forgotten, chikan had become a symbol of the exploitation of women whom society forbade to emerge from behind their veils to fight for their rights. SEWA started with one tin trunk, five women and a core investment of 10,000 rupees –many, many fears and much hesitation. Gradually the number of women grew as word spread of an organization which paid higher than market wages. The first two-room office became a meeting place where women shared not only work but also common concerns and companionship. Male hostility to new ways that threatened established norms disappeared as wives came home with much needed cash as well as liberated ideas.

The SEWA women travelled all over India in search of new markets: interacting and exchanging ideas with export buyers from Habitat and Bloomingdales, social activists and prime ministers. Today, over 7000 SEWA women share not just a turnover of several crore but a common commitment to quality and caring. They have discovered the fellowship of craftsmanship with tribals and Brahmins, stayed in *dharamshalas* and YWCAs, attended the Beijing Conference, shared a fashion ramp with Ritu Kumar and Mary MacFadden, signed the Shah Bano petition, and cast off their rigidly stratified notions of religion, male supremacy and birth control along with their *burkhas*.

As Lakhnavi life is a composite culture, chikan is composite embroidery. Traditionally made up of 44 different stitches, at least 22 – variants of six basic stitch techniques – are known and practiced today. Some are done on the surface of the fine white lawn fabric, some underneath it, others tease and pull the warp and weft threads apart to create a net-like *jaali* pattern at the heart of the flowers or leaves that make up the motif. Their names – double star earring, cowrie shell, peacocks feather eye, grain of rice, grass blade – are both descriptive and poetic. They combine to form an exquisite, textured light and shade pattern of stylized flowers, fauna and foliage that is unique in its delicacy yet vibrant strength. *Daraz*, patterned cutwork seams, skilfully snipped in the shape of flowers, leaves, zigzag, or even the Awadhi fish emblem, sets off the fine embroidery on kurtas and caps.

Like so many Indian embroideries, chikankari is a manifestation of a woman's inner spirit and creativity triumphantly transcending the sadness and squalor of her surroundings and the limitations of her circumstance. Like a dragonfly's wing, its white-on-white gossamer textures reflect the light and shade of her life – its beauty and its fragile, transient nature.

A more in-your-face embroidery that is also a characteristic of U.P. and Lucknow is *zardozi*. Using gold and silver threads, with an occasional addition of coloured silks, this glitteringly resplendent embroidery is done on fabric stretched on a long rectangular table-like frame, usually by men. Two or three craftspeople sit at a single frame, working this intricate embroidery with hooked needles – piercing the cloth from the front, and pulling it with a hooked movement from the back – much as a cobbler does. Used traditionally for court regalia and robes, as well as ornamented hangings and spreads, zardozi embroidery is now an essential part of every bridal wardrobe; Swarowski crystals often replacing the more traditional metal sequins, and the delicate silver wire *mukesh* of yore.

Another typically Lucknow textile craft is the colourful satin patchwork that is used for quilts and ghararas (skirts) and edges formal dupattas. Minute triangular, diamond and semi-circular shapes are stitched together in geometric patterns finished with gold ribbon to create a lustrous and dramatic chiaroscuro of colours. Sadly, many of the craftswomen who used to practice this skill are now in sweatshops; machine-appliquéing baba-suits with Mickey Mouse and Donald Duck cutouts! But look out for the tie-dyed crinkle-dried muslin scarves that are the *piece de resistance* of the Lakhnavi washermen. They are starched, twisted counter-clockwise, dip-dyed in flaming pinks, purples and yellows, and topped off with *abrak*, a luminous talc that gives an iridescent gold dust effect. Dupattas star-studded with sequins of different shapes and sizes, or dotted with silver and gold mukesh also set off the white chikan summer outfits. Apart from its own textile crafts, Lucknow is also a centre for fine Benarsi sarees and Farrukhabad block prints, as well as the rougher textures of *khadi* and handloom from neighbouring Barabanki.

The silver jewellery of Lucknow, filigree, beaten or moulded, has a distinctive character of its own – *jhumka* earrings, chains, and necklaces have the same Mughal-influenced paisley and florette motifs as the embroideries. Brass, copper, silver and gold – hammered, beaten or cast, engraved, enamelled or repousse – have been used through the centuries all over India. Ewers, waterpots, vases, lamps and trays, in shapes consecrated by tradition to temple ritual or court ceremonial, or simply for bringing water from the village well. Every Indian city has a street in the bazaar dedicated to the sale of each specific metal and Lucknow is no exception. Crafts-people sit in their shops, and one can custom-order a specific shape or design. Each metal has its ascribed attribute: according to an ancient text, the *Kalika Purana,* gold 'removes the excesses of the three humours and promotes strength of vision', silver is 'favourable and inimicable to bile, but calculated to increase the secretion of wind and phlegm', bronze is 'agreeable and intellectual, but favourable to undue excitement of blood and bile', brass is 'wind-generating, irritating, hot, and heat and phlegm-destroying', iron is 'beneficial in overcoming dropsy, jaundice and anemia'!

A metal technique worth looking out for is the engraved and enamelled *meenakari* brassware of U.P. While its main centre is Moradabad, fine examples of the work can be found in Lucknow. Respectively known as *siakalam*, chikan and *marori* work, the design is chased on tinned brass, and filled in with black or coloured lacquer, applied with a hot tool. When polished, the coloured patterns, generally flowing arabesques of flowers and foliage, emerge out of the glittering metal in an intricate, glowing relief.

Less well-known, but stunningly subtle in its dramatic black and white, is the Lakhnavi version of *bidri*, the silver damascene work originating in the old Hyderabad state in Central India. There was a brief period, in the late 18th and early 19th century, when Lucknow craftsmen produced their own bidri metal ware. Occasionally using gold to replace the silver, and with more delicate trellis-like designs than the stylized floral motifs or bold geometric jaals of their Hyderabadi counterparts, silver wire is beaten into the engraved design on boxes, bowls and vases made of an alloy or copper, zinc and lead, treated with a solution of copper sulphate and saltpetre that turns it black. The silver motif shines out from its jetty backdrop – stars on a dark night.

Crinkled *chunhat* and abrak that only lasts one wash but gives so much pleasure. The exquisite, formalized ritual of eating paan, folded and presented on crossed palms, and the horrid, lurid blood-red betel stains that go with it. The courteous verbal jugglery and poetic conceits that accompany even the most trifling transaction and the inevitable unpunctuality and broken promises that ensue as a result. The plumed, tasselled *tongas* and the monstrous comic cross between a dinosaur and jeep that is Lucknow's version of an auto-rickshaw. The combination of a Hindu political majority and a dominantly Muslim culture. The irrepressible folly and the fading grandeur. All are part of Lucknow's unique charm and character. All must be understood, experienced and savoured.

The crafts, threatened, sometimes tacky and anachronistic, but nevertheless a legacy of distinctive and extraordinary skills, reflect the cross-currents and the culture, the problems and potential.

Afternoons in the kothas of Lucknow

VEENA TALWAR OLDENBURG

IN the days when I was tramping around in the alleys of Lucknow trying to capture the ineffable essence of this multi-layered city, I was led to a small group of old and young courtesans in Gulbadan's *kotha* near the Akbari Darwaza in Chowk. Over a decade (1976-86), in more than a score of meetings, I came to appreciate these powerful, alluring, independent, bold, even wild women. In conversations that were as hilarious as they were informative, they dismantled the clichés and prejudices that informed my view of them. They managed to stand my conventional opinions of courtesans and wives, of 'wicked' and 'normal' woman in the 'normal' world, slowly but surely on their head. These extraordinary women unveiled the secrets of the kotha, sharing with me their clandestine, devious, and intimate ploys for survival and economic independence, challenging the very 'respectability' of society's central pillar – marriage.

I pursued my fascination with the courtesans of Lucknow from their heyday at the Lucknow court, through the colonial period where they adapted and survived, to the virtual extinction of their profession for a lack of patronage in the seventies and eighties and competition from the song-filled creations of Bombay cinema.

Before I actually walked up the narrow stairs to the kotha, I came across the city's famous courtesans in the civic tax ledgers of 1858-77 and in the related official correspondence preserved in the Municipal Corporation record room in Lucknow. Listed as 'dancing and singing girls', it was astounding to discover that they were in the highest tax bracket, with the largest individual incomes of any in the city! Their names were also on lists of property – houses, orchards, manufacturing and retail establishments for food and luxury items – confiscated by British officials for their proven involvement in the siege of Lucknow and the rising against colonial rule in 1857. These women, though patently non-combatants, were penalized for their clandestine instigation of and pecuniary assistance to the rebels.

On yet another list, some 20 pages long and simply titled *'Loot'*, were recorded the spoils of war seized from one set of 'female apartments' in Qaisarbagh Palace, where some of the deposed king Wajid Ali Shah's innumerable (the number varies from 80 to upwards of 300 in various sources) consorts resided when the complex was seized by the British. It is a remarkable list and eloquently evocative of a very privileged existence: gold and silver ornaments studded with precious stones, embroidered cashmere wool and brocade shawls, bejewelled caps and shoes, silver, gold, jade and amber-handled fly whisks, silver cutlery, jade goblets, plates, spittoons, *hookahs*, and silver utensils for serving and storing food and drink, and valuable furnishings. The value of this extraordinary plunder was conservatively estimated at nearly four crore rupees (four million pounds sterling in 1857).

Courtesans dotted other colonial records as well. They appeared in frequent official memoranda written in connection with a grave medical crisis – that of rampant venereal diseases – that engulfed the military establishment in Lucknow, and all the 110 cantonments of British India. When European casualties during the mutiny and rebellion of 1857 were reckoned, it was discovered that more soldiers had died of disease than in combat. Compounding the shock of this discovery was the unspeakable horror of the fact that one in every four European soldiers was afflicted with a venereal disease. It quickly became clear that the battle to reduce European mortality rates would now be joined on the hygienic (read sexual) front, to ensure a healthy European army for the strategic needs of the Empire.

Ironically, it was the British soldiers who exposed these women (in their quarters in the Lal Bazaars of the cantonments) to venereal infections, like syphilis, that were previously unknown in India. Even more tragic, the medical establishment of British Raj never permitted a proper investigation into the cause of the venereal epidemic among European soldiers for fear of exposing the skeletons in their own closet. The doctors in-charge totally denied or hushed up homosexuality among the European soldiery. The brunt of this new war would be borne by the courtesans and prostitutes of Lucknow, along with those in the other cantonments in India. An omnibus law, enacted in 1864, made sure the profession was regulated and the women's bodies (mind you, not the bodies of the soldiers who were their clients!) were regularly inspected and controlled.

British political propaganda in the aftermath of revolt, however, did the greatest harm to the reputation of the kothas and its 'nautch girls' as they called them. The older *tawa'ifs*, who spoke keenly about contemporary politics, the law, and had connections among the local power elite, were equally well informed about the history of their city. In their view, the British had deliberately muddied the truth about their kothas in order to denigrate nawabi culture, and to gobble up Awadh. In a campaign waged against them to reduce their influence, the new government resumed control over much of the prime real estate given to them by the nawabs and other patrons. Yet, when it came to matters such as using these women as prostitutes for the European garrison, or collecting income tax, the eminently pragmatic Victorians set aside their high moral dudgeon, and decreed rules to enforce both.

It became official policy to select the healthy, light skinned and beautiful 'specimens' from among the kotha women, and arbitrarily relocate them in the cantonment for the convenience and health of the European soldiers. This not only dehumanized the profession, stripping it of its cultural function, but made sex cheap and exposed the women to venereal infection from soldiers, and passing it on in turn. The collective impact of the new legislation, the loss of court patronage, the confiscation of their lands and orchards and the fines extracted from the tawa'if for their role in the rebellion, was a severe blow to the courtesans and signalled the gradual debasement of a vital cultural institution into common prostitution.

These new challenges provoked these women to mount a sly counter-offensive to keep out a meddlesome civic authority that taxed their incomes and inspected their bodies. With characteristic audacity they responded by keeping two sets of books on their incomes, to pay less tax; they bribed the local *dai*, or nurse, to avoid bodily inspections. They kept the local policemen 'happy' with sex and money to avoid arrest for selling liquor to the soldiers, or publicly refused to pay taxes even when threatened with imprisonment. These tactics were new but the spirit behind them was veteran.

Back in the archives my accidental discovery of a stash of documents led me to a group of courtesans living in Lucknow in 1976. These documents were the intercepted letters written by Wajid Ali Shah in exile. I engaged a young Persian scholar, Chhote Mian, (a pseudonym) to help me decipher these Persian letters. He not only provided the entree required to visit this group of courtesans, but also, quite fortuitously, the key to comprehending their world. They were the proud, albeit less affluent, descendants of those who had survived first the pressures of a century of systematic harassment by the colonial authorities, and then the abolition of zamindari in 1952 that tightened the fists of their best patrons, and finally the total ban placed on their profession by the puritanical, if not outright hypocritical, government of independent India in 1957.

Chhote Mian explained why he had only been given a pet name instead of a serious Muslim family name. He was the son of a courtesan and she had never revealed to him who his father was. Ironically, his sad life-story had all the elements of the upbringing accorded to a girl in a 'normal' household:

'While I love and respect my mother and all my "aunts" [other courtesans] and my grandmother [a chaudhurayan], my misfortune is that I was born a son and not a daughter in their house. When a boy is born in the kotha, the day is without moment, even one of quiet sadness. When my sister was born there was a joyous celebration that was unforgettable. Everyone received new clothes, there was singing, dancing, and feasting. My aunts went from door to door distributing laddoos [a sweet traditionally distributed to mark an auspicious event]. The musicians were drunk and received expensive gifts.

'My sister is today a beautiful, educated, propertied woman. She will also inherit what my mother and grandmother own. She will have a large income from rents; she doesn't even have to work as a courtesan, if she so chooses. I am educated, but I have no money or property. Jobs are very hard to come by, so I live in a room and live on a small allowance that my mother gives in exchange for running errands for her and helping her deal with her lawyers. [She was trying to evict a tenant from a house she owned.] She paid for my education but a college degree is pretty worthless these days. My only hope is that I may marry a good woman who has money and who gives me sons so they can look after me in my old age, or find a way of getting a job in Dubai, as my cousin did. Otherwise my chances in life are pretty dim. Funny isn't it, how these women have made life so topsy-turvy?'

This inversion in a society that blatantly favours sons over daughters left me bewildered, although the tawa'ifs had the answers.

The courtesans had established themselves as an influential group of women under the lavish patronage of the chief noblemen, merchants, and the official elite. Abdul Halim Sharar, a novelist and journalist who chronicled the history of the nawabs of Awadh and their cultural innovations, writes that in Lucknow, association with the courtesans started with the reign of Shuja ud Daula (reigned: 1753-1774). It became fashionable for the noblemen to associate with some bazaar beauty, either for pleasure or for social distinction. A cultivated man like Hakim Mahdi, who later became Wazir (prime minister of

Awadh), owed his initial success to a courtesan named Piyaro, who advanced her own money to enable him to make an offering to the ruler on his first appointment as Governor of a Province of Awadh. These absurdities went so far that it is said that until a person had association with courtesans he was not a polished man. At the present time (circa 1920) there are still some courtesans with whom it is not reprehensible to associate, and whose houses one can enter openly and unabashed. Although these practices may have a deteriorating effect on the morals, at the same time manners and social finesse improved.

Ensconced in sumptuous apartments in the bazaars of Chowk, and in the Qaisarbagh, they commanded great respect in the court and in society, were frequent performers at the palaces of the nawabs and the nobility, and association with them bestowed prestige on those who were invited to their salons for cultural soirees. It was not uncommon for the young sons of the nobility to be sent to the best-known salons for instruction in etiquette, the art of conversation, appreciation of Urdu poetry, and even the finer points of love-making. They were the recognized preservers and performers of the high culture of the court and actively shaped the developments in Hindustani music and Kathak dance styles. Their style of entertainment was widely imitated in other Indian court cities, and their more recent influence on the Hindi films is all too patent. The popularity of Indian films rests chiefly on their songs and dances. The very notion of the romantic musical owes its inspiration to the style of entertainment at the kotha, and several tawa'ifs and their daughters, including Jaddan Bai and her later famous daughter Nargis, found work in Bombay in the budding film industry.

Gulbadan's kotha was bustling with life when I arrived. I was shown around, and my queries and silences were met with loquacious explanations. The owner and manager of the kotha was the *chaudharayan*, or chief courtesan, an older woman who has retired to the position of manager after a successful career as a tawa'if. Gulbadan had acquired wealth and fame, and she recruited and trained the girls who came for their various reasons, along with the more talented daughters of the household. Typically, a wealthy courtier, (and during the nawabi, often the king himself), began his direct association with a kotha by bidding for a virgin whose patron he became with the full privileges and obligations of that position. He was obliged to make regular contributions in cash and jewellery, privileged to invite his friends to soirees, and to enjoy an exclusive sexual relationship with a tawa'if. His guests were expected to impress the management with their civilities and substance so that they would qualify as patrons of the women who were still unattached, or at least as 'regulars' of the kotha.

The chaudharayan always received a fair chunk of the earnings to maintain the apartments, pay to hire and train other dancing girls, and attract gifted tabla and sarangi players, chefs, and special servants that such establishments employed. Many of the musicians belonged to famous lineages and much of late-19th-century Hindustani music was invented and transformed in these salons, to accommodate the taluqadars and new professional men who filled the patronage vacuum in the colonial period.

Other women, called *thakahi* and *randi*, were affiliates of a kotha but had little or no prestige. Their less remarkable appearance and talent restricted them to providing sexual services in their spartan quarters downstairs. Secretly associated with the establishment were *khangi*, or women who were married and observed strict *purdah*, but who, for financial or other reasons came to the kotha for clandestine liaisons; the chaudharayan collected a fee from them for her hospitality. A large number of men were also employed as doormen, watchmen, errand boys, tailors, palanquin carriers and others, as was her grandson, Chhote Mian, who had brought me there. They lived on the lower floors of the house or in detached servants' quarters and were also often kinsmen who screened suspicious characters at the door, acted as protectors of the house, and spied on the activities of the police and medical departments. Pimps or other male agents came into existence in the colonial period, but Gulbadan had managed to keep them at bay. She also disabused me of some entrenched myths about the kotha.

The notion that the chaudharayan's recruitment practices were and are shady and unscrupulous has become well-established over time. It is popularly believed that the most common mode of recruitment was, and still is, kidnapping; that the tawa'ifs were linked to a large underground network of male criminals who abducted very young girls from villages and small towns and sold them to the kothas or *nishat khanas* (literally, pleasure houses). Lucknow's famous poet and litterateur, Mirza Hadi Ruswa, romantically fuelled, if not actually generated, this belief in his *Umrao Jan Ada.* The novel first appeared in 1905 and was an immediate best seller; the fictional Umrao Jan became the quintessential tawa'if of Lucknow. Set in the second half of the 19th century, it is a melodramatic story of Umrao Jan, who as a beautiful child of five is kidnapped and sold to a tawa'if in Lucknow, where she trains and becomes, after a few complicated twists and turns in the plot, a renowned and much sought-after courtesan. Ruswa uses the classic ploy of writing an introduction wherein he explains that he is merely recording the true story of Umrao Jan, told to him by the protagonist herself. His use of the first person in the 'memoir', in which the courtesan frequently addresses him by name, makes it all the more convincing.

The myth about kidnapping was stoutly punctured as I conversed with roughly 30 women, whose ages ranged from 35 to 78, and a more nuanced picture emerged. The compelling circumstance that brought a majority of them to the various tawa'if households in Lucknow was the misery they endured in either their natal or their conjugal homes. Four of these women were child widows, two of whom hailed from the same district and had lost their husbands in a cholera epidemic; three were sold by their parents when famine conditions made feeding these girls impossible. Seven were victims of physical abuse, two of whom were sisters regularly beaten by their alcoholic father for not obliging him by making themselves sexually available to the toddy-seller. Three were known victims of rape and deemed unmarriageable; two of them had left their ill-paid jobs as municipal sweeper-women, because they were tired of 'collecting other people's dirt', two were battered wives, one had left her husband because he had a mistress, and one had run away for her love for music and dancing that was not countenanced in her orthodox Brahmin home. Three said they had left their husbands without much ado, seeing the advantage of earning their own living and being at liberty to use their resources as they wished, and did not want to have children. The remaining four were daughters of other tawa'ifs. Not one claimed that kidnapping had been her experience, although they had heard of such cases. This assortment of refugees from the *sharif*, or respectable, world gave a completely ironic slant to the notion of respectability.

The problem, according to Saira Jan, a plump, good-looking woman in her early forties who recounted her escape from a violent and alcoholic husband with humour, was that there were no obliging kidnappers in her *muhalla* (neighbourhood). 'Had there been such *farishte* [angels] in Hasanganj, I would not have had to plot and plan my own escape at great peril to my life.'

This catalogue reflects the wide range of unfavourable, even dangerous, circumstances from which these women had escaped. Desertion has been traditionally resorted to by those trapped in situations they had no other effective means of fighting or changing. Gulbadan, who had become the chaudharayan in her late thirties (she claims she was born in c. 1900 and initiated – *nath uteri* – when she was 13 years old), had been the niece of a tawa'if and was raised in the household she now managed. She spoke of the kotha as a sanctuary for both men and women; men escaped the boredom of their domestic lives and women found in it a greater peace and freedom than in the normal world. She reminded Saira that she was a miserable, underweight, frightened wretch when she had first appeared at her doorstep.

'She was thin as a stick, her complexion was blotchy, her eyes sunk in black holes, and she had less than two rupees tied to the end of her sari. Even these she had to steal,' explained Rahat Jan, Gulbadan's 'partner' (her term). 'Now look at her, we call her our *hathini* [female elephant], who eats milk and *jalebi* [syrup-filled, deep fried sweets] to keep herself occupied between meals, although she argues it is to keep her voice melodious.'

Most women told stories of their prior lives without inhibition. They had wanted to escape 'hell' (the word *jahannum*, the Islamic hell, was frequently used to describe their earlier homes) at any cost. The rigours of learning professional skills, chaste Urdu, and earning their own money helped them develop self-esteem and value the relative independence they encountered in Gulbadan's and Rahat Jan's kotha. Here they could be women first, and Hindus and Muslims in a more mutually tolerant way, since the culture of the kotha represented elements of both, and was acknowledged as a true example of the Ganga-Jamuni tehzeeb.

The story of one of the Hindu child widows, Rasulan Bai, 35, is especially compelling because it exposes the ineffectiveness of the 150 years of social-reform legislation and the lack of options for young childless widows even today. While it is the story of a seasoned rebel, it also explains why a courtesan does not consider herself complicit in bolstering values that keep other women in powerless positions:

'I was married when I was ten in a land-owning Rajput family where my mother did not work. Born in Lucknow, I attended three years of school but I barely knew how to recognize the letters that spell my name. My *gauna* ceremony occurred just three months after I began menstruating. I remember arriving at my husband's house with my dowry, and plenty of gifts for my in-laws. That summer [1960] there was a very big flood, which drowned most of the city, destroyed our house, livestock and our food reserves. While my husband was out with his brothers trying to salvage some of the food stored in earthenware jars, he drowned. I survived but I often wished I were dead.

'The local Brahmin said that my ill-starred presence had brought flood and death to the city. My jewels, clothes, and the few silver coins which I had hidden away, were forcibly taken away from me, and I became a widow in white who did all the nasty, heavy chores for the household. I was thrown scraps when I cried out in hunger. You talk about the laws that were passed by the British to prevent child marriage, you talk of the rights we won [the Hindu Civil Code, 1956] but I scoff at all that. I had no recourse to laws or to lawyers, only to my wits sharpened by adversity. I first tried to get back at them with sly acts of sabotage. I did the washing-up indifferently, leaving a dull film on the metal platters and the pots. For this my mother-in-law thrashed me. I would sneak into the kitchen when my sister-in-law had finished cooking and add a heavy dose of salt to the lentils and vegetables. I would hide my smile when I heard the yells and abuse heaped on her by the men folk. She caught me and thrashed me till I was unconscious.

'Life was unbearable but I was trapped; there was nowhere that I could go. My parents, who had come for the funeral, were distressed but they did not offer to take me back because they still had my younger sisters to marry. Fights, violence erupted all the time. Finally, when they found out that I stole money to buy snacks from the vendor, they threatened to burn me alive. I wanted to run away but didn't know where I would go, except to the Gomti to drown myself. Eventually, I found shelter with a troupe of itinerant performers after I told them my troubles and showed them the bruises on my body. They smuggled me out of that hell, gave me bit parts in their dramas, and finally brought me to the lap of Bibi Khanum [another tawa'if] in Lucknow, and I have never looked back. I had no option but to run away. Tell me, sister, what would you have done in my place?'

There were many stories, each with its own flavour of horror, and of courage.

'Many women flee their homes in the villages, and come to the anonymity of the city to work as domestic servants, as ayahs or maids, or cooks,' said Gulbadan as she tucked another paan into her mouth. 'Some join road gangs run by government or private building contractors only to break bricks into small pieces with a hammer, all day in the sun, and earn in a month what we make in a few hours of passing the time in civilized company. To make ends meet they have to sleep with their employers and the *dalals* [middlemen], who found them their jobs, and get beaten up by their husbands when they find out. A woman compromises her dignity twenty-four hours of the day when she has no control over her body or her money.' This response was peppered by the remarks of the others, who agreed that women are always vulnerable to the exploitative demands of men in the outside world.

The women who said that their own parents had sold them when they were unable to feed them, let alone set aside money to pay for a wedding and a dowry, felt that their parents were forced by circumstances to take such a heartless decision. Now they sent money home every month to take care of their impoverished families, which was gratefully received, and whatever resentment they may have felt for being abandoned as children had dissipated through understanding the limits imposed on women in this world. Gulbadan, who spoke more aphoristically than the others, said she had grown old and withered in her three score and ten years but the scope for women to change the lives they grumblingly led was minuscule.

What they couldn't change they called their fate, their *kismat*, their *naseeb*. Here, in our world, even though things are not as good as they were before the angrez came, women change their fate. Even philosophers and poets will tell you that no one can change their kismat. Ask these women, who have lived and worked together for more than 20 years, whether or not they think that I taught them how to mould their own fate like clay with their own hands.

I did, and they agreed, with laughing nods, while they celebrated Janam Ashtami (birthday of the Krishna, the divine patron of Kathak) and the Muslim festival of Eid on the third floor of Gulbadan's impressively large building.

Gulbadan had tossed this off as she sat on the large platform covered with an old Persian rug and worn velvet-and-brocade bolsters that propped her up. Watching her deft fingers prepare a paan, or betel leaf, with its half dozen nut-and-spice fixings, I felt I was in the presence of an alchemist who had transformed base fortunes into gold. She, along with her septuagenarian friends, had inherited a way of life and struggled to preserve it, quite selfishly, in the face of an increasingly hostile future. Their business was neither to exploit women, nor to transform the lot of the generality of womankind, but to liberate and empower themselves and those with whom they were associated.

The high level of camaraderie, banter, and affectionate interaction that I observed and participated in on several visits to their apartments over eight years affirmed this impression repeatedly. The chaudharayan enacts several roles, the most challenging being to inspire, in the women who come to them, a confidence in their own ability and worth, restore shattered nerves and set about undoing the inferiority they had internalized. Saira helpfully explained:

'The problem was to forget the meaning of the word *aurat* [woman] that had been dinned into my mind from the day I was born. Fortunately I was still a child [eleven or twelve] so forgetting was not as difficult as it might have been even a few years later. I forgot my misery upon arriving in a house where a different meaning for that word was already in place, where Amina Bai and Zehra Jan [Gulbadan's granddaughters] were acting out those meanings for us all.

'They did not fear men because they were admired and praised by men; nor had they dealt with nagging mothers and aunts about not doing this, or that. They never worried about not being able to get married, nor scolded or slapped by their fathers for being "immodest". The shadow of *dahej* [dowry] had never darkened their lives. I resented them to begin with, thought them spoilt and selfish, but slowly I began to realize that they were of a different ilk. I would have to break my own mental mould and recast myself. I got a lot of love from Gulbadan, Rahat Jan, and Amiran. They would listen to me, and I would regurgitate all the sorrow, pain, and poison I had swallowed, again and again. Now when I tell you my story, it is as if I am telling you another's tale. Really, I didn't know that I was capable of doing anything, being anyone, or owning my own building and employing seventeen carpenters in a *charpai karkhana* [wooden cot workshop]. I had the mentality of a timid and ugly mouse; now I am accused of being too arrogant, and am envied for the property I own.'

The self-fashioning ethos of the kotha, quarrels and jealousies notwithstanding, makes it possible for them to assimilate their newly revised perceptions and behaviour patterns. They mostly agreed that living among a host of nurturing women (and even with some who were not) without the dread of men, and freedom from the pressure of the 'marriage market' where grooms were 'for sale', gave them the inner courage to develop their skills and perceive themselves the equals of men.

There are other therapeutic devices invented over the ages that are still in use in these salons. The novices assimilate a secret repertoire of satirical and bawdy songs, dances, mimicking, miming and dramatic representations, aimed at the institution of marriage and heterosexual and homosexual relations that are privately performed only among women. These 'matinee shows', as they call them, help 'the newcomers to discard the old and internalize the new meaning of being an aurat.' I recognized this, when in answer to one of my early (and very naive) questions I was treated to a improvised vignette, '*Shaadi ya barbaadi*?' (marriage or disaster?).

VTO: Gulbadan, since you are a handsome woman, so well educated, with all this money and property and jewels, why didn't you marry a well-to-do man and settle down to a life of respectability?

Gulbadan (first frowned pensively, and then laughingly said): We first thought you were a *jasoos* [spy] for the government or the Christian missionaries; Chhote Mian tells me you visit their offices all the time with your notebook. *Par aap to bilkul nadaan* [naïve] *hain.* You ask strangely ignorant questions, which you call doing *Amriki* [American] research. Is marriage 'respectable' in Amrika? Are women not abused there? Do they not divorce? Well let us show you what marriage is before you wish it on an old and respectable woman like me, or any of us here. Let us dispel the darkness in your mind about the nature of marriage.

Of what they then played out for me, I can only offer a prosaic summary, because it is difficult to capture the visual thrill of the half-hour-long satirical medley of song, dance, dialogue and mime that followed: A wailing sarangi was the perfect substitute for the sound of an unhappy wife. Rasulan immediately took her dupatta (long scarf) and wound it around her head as a turban to play the husband. Elfin Hasina Jan took her cue as the wife; others became children and members of the extended family, while Gulbadan remained on her settee amid the bolsters, taking occasional drags from the *hookah*, presiding, as a particularly obnoxious mother-in-law, on a scene of domestic turmoil.

Hasina Jan playing wife and mother first surveys the chaos: the children meul, ask for food and drink, and want to be picked up. The mother-in-law orders that her legs, which have wearied from sitting, be massaged; the husband demands food and undivided attention; the father-in-law asks for his *hookah chillum* to be refilled, and a sister-in-law announces that she cannot finish doing the laundry, nor knead the *chapati* dough because she is not feeling too well. Hasina is defeated, harried, and on the brink of a nervous breakdown. While muttering choice obscenities under her breath she begins, in a frenzied way, to do the job of a wife. She lights the coal stove, dusts and tidies the room, cooks, presses the legs of the mother-in-law who emits pleasurable grunts, carries live coals to replenish the hookah, tries to soothe baby who is now snivelling, puts plates of food in front of the demanding husband. She nearly trips another bawling child. She finally collapses, striking her brow with her hand as she croaks a '*hai tobah*' ('never more').

A little later the din subsides and she, choked with sobs, says that her kismat is terrible, that she will jump into the well to escape her fate. She is chained to this frightful life, all for the sake of money to fill her stomach and for shelter. The rest of the household snores noisily. Her husband, who is belching and hiccupping after his food and drink, makes a lunge at her for some quick sex. She succumbs, and after 30 agitated seconds of his clumsy effort, she asks him for money for household expenses. He grudgingly parts with 20 rupees, reminding her that she needs to restock his supply of the local brew. She complains that the money is just not enough even for the groceries, for which she receives a slap, tearfully renders an accounting of the money she spent last week, cries some more and finally falls asleep, wretched and hungry. 'So wives don't do it for money,' Saira giggled, giving me a nudge in my ribs, 'they are selflessly serving society.' There is not a dry eye in the audience; we have tears of laughter streaming down our faces. So, jested another in English: 'Will you be a wife or tawa'if?'

They had transmuted grim reality into parody. The thankless toil of an average housewife, including her obligation to sexually satisfy a sometimes faithless, or alcoholic, or violent husband, for the sake of a very meagre living came across vividly. 'Was not the situation of the housewife tantamount to that of a common prostitute, giving her body for money? It is we who are brought up to live in *sharafat* [genteel respectability] with control over our bodies and our money and they who suffer the degradation reserved for lowly [*neech*] women,' Saira added, lest I, poor naïve thing, had missed the whole point of their theatricals.

Such vivid irony is a stock idiom in their speech and song. Male in-laws, particularly fathers and brothers-in-law, are caricatured in countless risqué episodes enacted regularly and privately among women. As things got more raucous I began to think that even their refined speech – *begamati zubaan* – seemed to be an affect. They ridiculed the aggression and brevity of sexual arousal in men, even as they amuse, educate, and edify the denizens of the kotha. These routines, embellished with their peculiarly rude brand of humour, irreverent jokes and obscene gestures, are performed like secret anti-rites, distilled and transmitted from generation to generation as their precious oral heritage.

I had also seriously questioned the courtesans' use of the *burqa*. This cloak, usually black or white, is worn over regular clothes and covers the wearer from head to foot, extending the seclusion of Muslim women, who observe purdah outside the home. The wearers see the world through a small rectangular piece of netting that fits over the eyes, while they remain hidden. Indubitably an artefact of a male-dominated society, where men dictate that women keep themselves covered so as not to provoke lewd comments or lustful aggression. I was baffled at why tawa'ifs not only used the burqa to move around when they went visiting or shopping since injunctions about female modesty did not apply to them, but also insisted that I should wear one as they led me to other kothas in the vicinity.

It was precisely because they were not required to be in purdah, they reasoned (in another classic reversal of patriarchal logic), that they chose to block the gaze of men. It was an extension of the autonomy they enjoyed in their living space and their *jism* (bodies), unlike 'normal' women whose bodies were considered the property of their husbands. They were forced to remain in seclusion to maintain (and increase) *khaandaani izzat*, or family honour; for them to show their faces in public would bring disgrace to their families. 'Ah, but our case is just the opposite,' said Saira. 'Men long to see our faces. If they could brag among their friends that they had seen Gulbadan or Amiran in the bazaar without a covering, they would go up in the esteem in which their friends hold them. We are not in the business of giving them cheap thrills. While we walk freely and anonymously in public places, looking at the world through our nets, they suffer deprivation because we have blinkered them. As you know by now, we do not bestow anything on men without extracting its price.'

I would have disputed this had I not experienced the temporary freedom the burqa gave me to walk along the winding alleys in a very old-fashioned and gossip-filled city, where I formerly never passed without being accosted with vulgar taunts from the idle youth who mill on the streets. These women had appropriated the power of the gaze while eluding the leer of sexually frustrated men. Playing by the rules of strict segregation practised in the old parts of Lucknow to keeps strangers from being aroused at the sight of 'respectable women', the tawa'ifs find the burqa liberating instead of restrictive, and are aggressively invisible to all those who wish to behold their faces. They know they can discard the burqa at will, as some of the younger women in the outer world are doing in defiance more and more, but they choose to use it as a perforated barrier between the world and them. Yet its use remains an indictment of male behaviour and culture.

While I had heard about the rigorous training and education courtesans undergo to ultimately please and entertain their patrons, I was to learn, for the first time, of their secret weapon – the art of *nakhra,* or pretence. Courtesans master the skill of duping their patrons in order to spare no opportunity of coaxing money out of them and their friends. In addition to their exorbitant rates, they subtly deploy an arsenal of devious 'routines' that make up the sly subtext of an evening's entertainment, to bargain, cajole, and extort extra cash or kind from their unsuspecting patrons. Some of these are practiced, some invented, but nuances are refigured with care to suit the temperament of a client or the mood of the moment to always appear 'spontaneous'.

These well-rehearsed ploys – the feigned headache that interrupts a dance or a song, pretend sulking and pouting, an artificial limp that prevents a dance, tears, a jealous rage – have beguiled generations of *rais*, the rich, to transfer their wealth to these women. The tawa'ifs refusal, at a critical juncture, to complete a sexual interlude with a favourite patron is a particularly profitable device, because affected coital injuries or painful menstrual cramps involve expensive and patient waiting on the part of the patron. Gulbadan said she often carried the game a step further by 'allying' herself with the patron against the 'offending' courtesan to lend credibility to the scene. She would scold and even slap her until the patron begged her not to be so harsh. Gulbadan was the privately acclaimed champion of these more serious confidence tricks, and others cheerfully confessed to having blackmailed, stolen, lied and cheated for material gain as soon as they acquired competence in this art. They invest their gains shrewdly to retire comfortably at the age of 35 – when beauty begins to fade and thicker midriffs make dancing an unpretty sight.

The formula, Gulbadan confided, is to win the complete trust of the man. This they do by first mastering all the information about the man – his public reputation, his finances, his foibles and vanities, his domestic relationships and any embarrassing secrets: 'Then,' giving me a naughty wink and making a grasping gesture, 'you have them by their short and curlies.' She continued:

'Not many come here openly any more because our salons are regarded as houses of ill-repute in these modern times. Most come only to drink or for sex, both in short supply at home. We know how to get a man drunk and pliant, so that we can extort whatever we want from him: money, even property, apologies, jewels, perfume, or other lavish gifts. Industrialists, government officers, other businessmen come here now; they have a lot of black money [undeclared cash] that they bring with them, sometimes without even counting it. We make sure that they leave with very little, if any. We know those who will pay large sums to ensure secrecy, so we threaten them with careless gossip in the bazaar or with an anonymous note addressed to their fathers or their wives.

'We do not act collectively as a rule but sometimes it may become necessary to do so. We once did a drama, against a moneylender who came and would not pay us the money he had promised for holding an exclusive soiree for him. So when a police officer, who had fallen in love with me, came by, we all told him tales of how the wretched man would not return jewels some of us had pawned with him. We filed a police report, he was arrested, and some of the pawned items (which the jeweller had taken from some of our recently straitened noble patrons) were made over to us by the lovelorn officer; others of his debtors sent us gifts and thanks for bringing the hated Rastogi to justice.

'But our biggest nakhra of all is the game of love that makes these men come back again and again, some until they are bankrupt. They return every evening, like the flocks of homing pigeons, in the vain belief that it is we who are in love with them.'

Umrao Jan, Ruswa's alleged confidante, presents this particular nakhra insightfully:

'I am but a courtesan in whose profession love is a current coin. Whenever we want to ensnare anyone we pretend to fall in love with him. No one knows how to love more than we do: to heave deep sighs; to burst into tears at the slightest pretext; to go without food for days on end; to sit dangling our legs on the parapets of wells ready to jump into them; to threaten to take arsenic. All these are parts of our game of love. *But I tell you truthfully, no man ever really loved me nor did I love any man.*' (Emphasis added.)

A discussion of this last nakhra, which occurred only after several visits, brought perhaps their most startling secret to light. It was difficult to imagine that these women, even though they were economically independent, educated, and in control of their lives, would spurn the opportunity for real intimacy and emotional and sexual fulfilment. Everyone agreed that emotional needs do not disappear with success, fame, or independence; on the contrary, they often intensify. Almost every one of the women with whom I had private conversations during these many visits claimed that their closest emotional relationships were among themselves, and eight of them reluctantly admitted that their most satisfying erotic involvements were with other women. They referred to themselves as *chapat baz* or lesbians, and to *chapti*, or *chipti*, or *chapat bazi*, or lesbianism (after Shaikh Qalandar Bakhsh Jur'at, an Urdu poet from Lucknow, 1749-1809, wrote in rekhti, his now famous *Chapti Namah*). They seemed to attach little importance to labels, and made no verbal distinctions between homosexual and heterosexual relations. There was no other 'serious' or poetic term for lesbianism, so I settled for their colloquialisms.

Their explanation for this was that emotions and acts of love are gender free. Normal words for love such as *mohabbat* (Urdu) or *prem* (Hindi), or love (English) are versatile and can be used to describe many kinds of love, such as the love of man or woman, the love for country, for siblings, parents of either sex. There was, in their view, no need to have a special term for love between two women, nor was there a need to flaunt this love in any way. There are words that suggest passionate love, like *ishq*; and are used by either gender. Although their bisexuality was a strictly private matter for them, the absence of a specialized vocabulary reduced it to a simple fact of their liberal lives, like heterosexuality, or the less denied male homosexuality. The lack of special vocabulary can be interpreted as the ultimate disguise for it; if something cannot be named it is easy to deny its existence. Urdu poetry, too, is often ambiguous about gender, and homosexual love often passes for heterosexual love. Many poems really express homosexual love, of the persona of the poem for a young boy, who is described in the idioms for feminine beauty.

The frank discussions on the subject of their private sexuality left some of my informants uneasy. I had probed enough into their personal affairs, they insisted, and they were not going to satisfy my curiosity any further; they were uncomfortable with my insistence on stripping bare their strategic camouflage, by which they also preserved their emotional sanity. Their diffidence to talk about their lesbianism underscores their quiet but profound subversion of social values. It became clear that for many of them heterosexuality itself is the *lajawab nakhra*, the ultimate artifice, credibly packaged with contrived passion and feigned orgasms. My ardour for precise statistics faded as the real meaning of their silences and their disguises began to sink in.

'I know, I know,' continued Afsar Jan, impatiently, 'we are blamed for enabling men to maintain their double moral standards and destroying happy marriages. Must we betray our own interests for the dubious cause of women who suffer such men as husbands, fathers, and brothers? Today, things are grim; Lucknow's landed gentry lost their power after zamindari was abolished, and our profession is now illegal; there is hardly a handful of kothas in operation. Has this helped the cause of women or only made life harder for us? Are men treating their wives better? Beating them less? Only we have been silenced and we are now invisible in Lucknow society.'

In fact their silence is so well held that, for all official intents and purposes (such as taxation), the prudish administration's own nakhra is that it has abolished the world's oldest profession. Yet, climbing up the rickety stairs of the now seedy kothas in the alleys of Lucknow's Chowk are the new patrons, petty shopkeepers and a large number of public officials, not for an engaging cultural soiree but for some furtive, loveless sex. For the tawa'if it is a mixed outcome: it is a small triumph, because their incomes, although barely adequate, are no longer taxed; it is a larger defeat because officialdom can piously claim that it has banned female sexual exploitation.

This completed the century long process of converting a proud cultural institution into a species of 'vice' and Lucknow's celebrated kothas into musty dens for furtive sexual encounters.

A mesh of memories

NASIMA AZIZ

GOING home to Lucknow between Foreign Service assignments with my husband was always hurried and rushed. Post retirement, I have plenty of time at last. I have a deep need to reconnect with my childhood, my place, and to come to terms with the loss of people who are gone forever.

I spent six wonderful months in Lucknow meeting Lakhnavis from every walk of life, letting them talk to me about how life was lived – all those memories, myths and legends – a nostalgia binge that soothes my restless memory genes...

I have recorded these stories just as people recalled them, and just as they were told to me. In this selection of interviews connecting threads link seven amazing women: Mahé Talat, Betty, Manju, Hamida, Sakina, Shamim and Rana. My deepest thanks for their time and for photos provided.

I am heading towards Nakkhaas, a wide avenue in Old Lucknow, once famous for its elegant town houses. By the time I was growing up, Nakkhaas was better known for the weekly bazaar where quixotic junk and exotic birds were sold. On one occasion we met a gentleman from Arizona who was looking for 'fighting cocks' to take back to improve his breeds. While cock fights are now banned, the antiques bazaar still continues.

I locate a tall doorway, painted red, with the name Afzal Mahal above it in Urdu and enter a courtyard with a guava tree and a water tap. The deep arches of a baradari *enclose one side; a steep, curving staircase leads to the roof top. Fresh whitewash gives a well kept look, with touches of soft green on doors, windows and trellises. I sit on a* charpai, *string bed, and wait for Mahé Talat, the lady I have come to meet. She is visible through the open arches of the baradari, teaching a group of young girls how to read and write. Their clothes are faded and shapeless, but their faces, beyond the weariness, are eager.*

Mahé Talat's story: 'I retired recently from the post of Librarian in Karamat Hussain Girls College. Now I tutor these poor girls. Literacy may give them a way out of their hopeless lives.

I was born in 1939 in this very house – Afzal Mahal. My mother was extremely ill during childbirth and there was gossip that she was poisoned. The English lady-doctor, Dr. Marchant, thought differently, and said she could save either me or my mother and although eventually both of us survived, I was taken away and given to Rani Shehenshah Begum, who brought me up. She was a close relation of my father and I considered her my *par-dadi* (great-grandmother).

She was the greatest influence in my life. She told me wonderful stories, including stories from Shakespeare.

Shehenshah Begum was the daughter of a Turk, Ramzan Ali Khan, whose mansion stood on the banks of the Gomti not far from the Residency, an area now occupied by the Haathi Park. Ramzan's sister, a Turkish princess, Sangi Khanum, was the wife of Nawab Saadat Ali Khan who ruled Awadh from 1798 to 1814. Ramzan Ali Khan was his prime minister.

In 1857, when Shahenshah Begum was barely five years old, the British cannons brought their mansion tumbling down. Ramzan Ali Khan died, though the circumstances are not clear. All that remains in that locality is a small mosque known as the Jinnaat wali Masjid, the mosque where *jinns* pray.

The family escaped in bullock carts to Malihabad. In time Shahenshah Begum and her sisters went on pilgrimage to the Shia holy places in Iraq and, like many others, they stayed on. This is where Shahenshah Begum grew up to become an elegant and highly educated woman, with arresting, bright blue eyes. She was exceptionally tall and wore size nine shoes.

In time a young Nawab came to Iraq on pilgrimage. He was Raja Nawab Fazle Ali Khan of the Akbarpur Riyasat in Awadh. He took Shahenshah Begum back to India as his bride.

In 1945/46, elections were held in our *mohalla*, and the polling booth was right outside Afzal Mahal. I was about six or seven years old but I remember that Lady Wazir Hasan came to our home and asked the women to come out and vote, assuring them that they would be safe in their *purdah*. My par-dadi stepped out of the house, looked around the street, staggered and fainted. As you can imagine there was such a commotion! She was brought back inside and I sat beside her, fanning anxiously. When she recovered she told me that it was the sight of the *Angrez* tommies on duty that gave her a shock. It reminded her of the time when she was a child, in 1857, and Angrez tommies stormed her father's house.

One day I remember asking my par-dadi why she was signing her name from left to right on some documents presented to her by emissaries from Akbarpur. She explained that it was the Devanagri script which she had learnt in the Akbarpur Riyasat. She knew six languages including Hindi, Urdu, Persian, Turkish, Arabic and English.

She died in 1952 at the age of 100 and needed a man-sized shroud for her burial.'

The next evening I am back in Afzal Mahal. Mahé Talat shows me around the baradari, a hall supported by pillared arches. It is now used as the living quarters with a dormitory-like arrangement of beds, except during

Mohurrum, the month of mourning in the Shia calendar, when it serves its original purpose of holding majlises, *religious meetings. The far wall has large, deep alcoves where* tazias, *religious symbols, are meant to be placed. We go back to sit in the courtyard, comfortably drinking tea. I lead Mahé Talat gently to talk about her childhood.*

'You want to know about my early life? What can I tell you – it was a wonderful childhood, growing up in this house, in this mohalla.

Afzal Mahal was originally owned by Husaini Khanum who during the Mutiny had also fled to Malihabad but was killed before she got there. I remember seeing her daughter whom we called Chunni Begum. She had by then gone mad, though she was still regal in her bearing. In 1901, the head of our family went to see a play by Agha Hasher Kashmiri, in the baradari of Afzal Mahal which was in a very broken-down condition and had been pawned to a Rastogi *mahajan*. Our family bought this Mahal, renovated it, and used the baradari for majlises again.

When the roof of the baradari was repaired they found multiple layers of clay pots, which kept the place cool. The present ceiling is not original – it is lower than the old one. The fish motifs that we have painted gold used to be in different shaded colours, in a degree of detail that is impossible to reproduce now. The beams appeared to be supported by porcelain *parees*, angels, with lifted arms. Lower down there were smaller parees set here and there supporting cornices. As a child I used to play with a slightly damaged one that had fallen off. It was my doll.

During Diwali there used to be a *mela*, fair, from Akbari Gate to Gol Darwaza. Particularly popular were clay toys which were models of the men and women of different professions – an idea that Wajid Ali Shah had suggested to the makers of the toys.

I remember the *Basant ki nau chandi* celebrations at the shrine of Shah Meena, which both Hindus and Muslims attended. Ain Ali was a famous eunuch with a long beautiful plait. From '50 to '54 I saw him dance in a procession, which included horses and elephants, on its way to the shrine.

No male servants were allowed inside our house. When the gardener came in to water the plants, he put a cloth on his head, an *andheri*. He was the one in purdah! Purdah was so strict that doctors and hakims had to pass the stethoscope or feel the pulse of the female patient across a curtain. I remember a very beautiful lady in her 70s, Shahida Jan, who observed purdah from people in any passing aeroplane up in the sky! My par-dadi was persuaded to sit for a portrait only after being assured that the photographer was in purdah since he had his face covered with a black cloth while he took her picture!'

I sit in the quiet courtyard, listening to Mahé Talat as the evening deepens to dusk, oblivious of the hum of traffic outside, carried away by the rhythm of a born storyteller who keeps her tone neutral, even as she describes some of the chilling and tragic circumstances of her life.

'So how did I end up working as a librarian in a college? Let me tell you how that happened.

I studied till Class III in Christ Church School. We used the King Reader, which was like the Radiant Reader that came later. One day I made the sign of the cross during a lightening storm. Alarmed, my parents withdrew me from that school and applied for admission in Talimgah-e-Niswan, a school for Muslim girls established by Begum Inam Habibullah. My mother and I went to call on her at her residence, 11 Mall Road, and for the occasion my mother wore a sari. The interview went off well and I joined the new school.

I used to spend hours in the library in our house. I read the translation of the *Tohra* and many other marvellous books. The books were of a very large size and a wide ribbon was needed to turn the pages. They were embellished with gold both outside and inside. I regularly read journals like *Khatoon* and we were encouraged to read the novels of Rashid-ul-Khairi. However, we were forbidden to read romantic novels like *Zakhme Ishq*

My father, Nawab Sultan Ali Khan, related to the Akbarpur family, had habits which needed money and more money. Over the years he sold all our treasures, all our possessions: books, paintings, furniture, even the bars of silver and gold that were kept for my dowry. He sold a walnut-wood screen to the Lucknow Museum – you can go and see it there!

Once when we were very young my father took my sister and me to visit his favourite *tawaif,* courtesan. I remember a very pretty lady, sitting on a high stool. The peacock embroidered on her *duputta* covered the side of her head. Musicians were gathered around. We were given *paan* folded with silver and gold *warq*, and innocently, I ate mine, but my sister became suspicious that it may contain poison and refused to eat hers. When we told our mother where we had been she was very angry and did not allow her husband into the house for many months.

The tawaifs had to keep their doors closed on Diwali and on Basant, when melas, fairs, were held in that area. Two well known tawaifs were Alla Rakhi who lived near Prakash Cinema and Naseem Jan of Calcutta who was related to Jaddan Bai, the mother of the film star Nargis. The film star Rehana lived near by in one of the lanes. She used to return to Lucknow for Mohurrum and organize a tazia procession, walking behind the tazia in her burqa.

When I was 14 years old my marriage was arranged to a 35 year old man – he was a Maulvi, so a trousseau was not expected. After I married him I found out that he had T.B. so whatever little money I did have was spent on his medicines. I had to nurse him and clean his slop bowls. It was a desperate life, lived in one single room, in which I had to cook as well. My husband died and I came back home. I was cleaned and disinfected and sent to bed. In those dark days I used to lock myself in my room with books as my only companions. I remember I read *Fasana-e-Ajaib* and *Fasana-e-Azad* during that time.

In the build up to Independence, we heard that in Lucknow University there were agitations which involved the poets Majaz, Ali Sardar Jaffrey, Shehenshah Saheb and others. We heard that students danced as they recited Majaz's poem: *Bol rey dharti bol*. Urdu newspapers such as *Sarfaraz* painted an alarming picture of what might happen to Muslims after independence. But there were no riots in Lucknow. It was due to the efforts made from the time of Wajid Ali Shah who created an atmosphere of friendship between Hindus and Muslims.

All my uncles left for Pakistan in 1947. In 1953 the Zamindari Abolition Act made people bankrupt overnight and many died of shock. My mother sent away the servants as we could not afford them. The rents from the shops (along the outer boundary wall of the house) were Rs 5 or Rs 10 per month.

Under these circumstances you can imagine how hard it was for me to find the money to take up my studies again. I did not want to go back to my old school so I chose to go to Karamat Hussain College which was called Muslim College in those days (1958). It was far away from my house. I arranged a rickshaw, wore my burqa and set out through fields and barren land to the other end of town. Miss Yusufzai and Miss Roshan Ara were my teachers. We wore uniforms, shalwar kameez, with dupattas made of a mulmul-like fabric called *jungle bari*, or a cheaper fabric called *mata phulan*. There must have been about 500 girls in my time.

I got my Bachelors degree in Library Science from Isabella Thoburn College. With my Bachelors degree in hand I felt I was someone of worth.

Sometimes I think I am glad that my father sold all that we owned – or I would have had to sell it myself. Instead, I was forced to find something of more lasting value – an education – by which I could support myself for the rest of my life.'

Betty and her husband Iqbal Ahmed Khan live in the Sadar area, near the Cantonment. The construction of roads, flyover and shops, and encroachment by thelawalas makes the approach to the house complicated. The original grounds of the house have been sold off in parcels over the years and a Nursing Home occupies one portion near the mosque. The front garden still remains, with attractive nooks and corners. Inside, the two exquisite antique carpets hanging on the walls of this huge, high-ceilinged living room do not succeed in reducing the barn-like proportions.

Betty's story: 'My father was Raja Nawab Yusuf Ali Khan of the Riyasat of Akbarpur in eastern U.P. One of his ancestors, a thaḳur, had wanted to marry a Muslim girl, so he converted to Islam and after that the family title became Thakur Nawab or Raja Nawab.

My father, Yusuf, enjoyed the luxurious life of a rich taluqdar's son. He went to Colvin Taluqdar College where, in those days, students had their own apartments with servants, a horse and a syce.

In Paris in the 1930s he met and almost married Amrita Sher Gill. The portrait that she painted of him hangs in the National Gallery of Modern Art in Delhi today.

I have a group photo taken in an elegantly furnished living room – the people in the photo are Amrita, her Sardar father and Hungarian mother, Yusuf, and the Hungarian man Amrita eventually married.

In 1937 Yusuf married my mother who was from a Mirza family from Bombay. I lost both my parents when I was quite young and being the sole heir of Akbarpur, was made a Ward of the Court and placed in the care of Justice Thomas and Lady Thomas. My real name is Ismat, and my pet name is Betty. I was sent to school in Woodstock in Mussoorie and later to I. T. College Lucknow (1952-55). To this day I try to attend the meetings of the Awadh Taluqdar's Association, because I have a right to be there. Akbarpur is the parliamentary constituency of the BSP leader Mayawati.

My father's father was Raja Nawab Ali Khan. He was a serious scholar of Indian classical music and was one of the founders of the Marris Music College, now called the Bhatkande College of Music. He had several Muslim wives, but then he fell in love with Isabella Thomas, sister of Justice Thomas, and married her. She had two daughters, Roshanara and Husnara, and a son, Yusuf, the only son of the Raja. Their home in Qaiserbagh, Akbarpur House, is now a bus depot.

Isabella had converted to Islam but after her husband died she and her two daughters became practicing Christians again. One married into a family in Lucknow called Mayadas, and another married an Englishman. But since Isabella's son Yusuf was the one and only heir, he remained a Muslim. Isabella died in 1948 or '49. My father's sisters have passed away but one of their children came to attend my son's wedding recently.

My father's grandfather was Raja Nawab Fazle Ali Khan. He was married to Rani Shehenshah Begum. She was a very regal and aristocratic-looking lady, very tall and fair, with blue eyes. She looked like the actress Veena who plays the role of Wajid Ali Shah's mother in the film Shatranj ke Khilari. She lived till the age of over 100 and died in 1952. In her lifetime she lost her husband, her only son and her only grandson (my father).

She lived by herself in a house called Afzal Mahal in Nakhkhas. Being alone, she called one of her relations from Akbarpur to come and live in her home with his wife and children. One of his daughters, Mahé Talat, still lives in that house.'

I am looking for a locality called Raja Bazar where the Rastogi Biradiri has been traditionally located. I take the road to Rakabgunj, up to the thana *of Agha Mir and from there enter Batashey Wali Gali, a narrow winding street bordered by grim, high walls inset with heavy doors. At the first crossing is the house called Bharat Ashram. I ring the bell. A servant opens the creaking, heavy bolts. I climb a few steep steps – and then a breathtaking surprise. An acre of greenery laid out in the style of a classic garden with a fountain in the middle. I cross the garden to reach Manju's part of the house. She welcomes me warmly and introduces me to various family members.*

Manju's story: 'My husband's grandfather was Lala Mohandas Rastogi. He was a moneylender, and his clients were the nawabs and taluqdars of Lucknow. He was a very wealthy man but also a philanthropist and gave *gupt-daan* to many charities.

My father-in-law was Babu Balabhdas Rastogi (1901-1970). He was one of the first graduates of Lucknow University, called Canning College in those days. He became a Gandhian – one day he collected all his fine clothes, pashminas and silks, and gave them away. He made one wing of this house into a library, open to all. It was well stocked with books, magazines and newspapers and in the evenings you could see people sitting on the benches in the garden, reading.

In our families we always used '*aap*' even while addressing servants. The driver was called 'Driver Saheb'. When my own daughter went to study design in Ahmedabad, being a well brought up Lakhnavi she used '*hum*' instead of '*main*'. Her colleagues used to tease her – how many of you? To say 'main' was considered aggressive and bad mannered. Wherever we go, people can tell from the way we speak that we are from Lucknow – from the politeness of our speech, as well as our manners. For example, I would never dream of giving someone something with my left hand – not only that, but we are taught that the left hand must support the right elbow while offering anything to a guest or elder.

My mother-in-law was very fond of using *itr*, perfume, when she got dressed for the evening. We used to greet guests by offering them small cotton balls soaked in itr which they placed behind their ears, or we sprinkled refreshing rose water on them from an elegant silver sprinkler.

There were a lot of cooking taboos in this Vaishnav family. The kitchen area consisted of several rooms having their own courtyard. Desserts changed with the seasons – *Andarsey ki goli* in the monsoon, and *Lowki ka lachcha* in summer. In summer we also served *sharbat* made of *khus*, *gulab* or *kewra* essence whipped into cold, sweetened milk. I remember the labels on the itr and essence bottles from the famous Asghar Ali Mohammed Ali perfume factory in Hina Building in Chowk.

My mother was also from the Rastogi *biradari*. Her father was a wealthy zamindar from Farrukhabad. Her family had land but they also lent money to the nawabs and rajas of U.P. and Rajasthan. They did not count money – they weighed it.'

The house on 11 Mall Road is more than 150 years old. I used to visit it as a child – I remember the semi-circular driveway bordered with sculpted trees of Chinese orange; a conservatory with swaying shadows and mysterious filtered light where a child could imagine a tropical adventure... today there is no driveway and no conservatory, only the encroachment of new construction. But the drawing room, with enormously high ceilings, takes you back to another time – and Hamida Habibullah enters, greeting me with her usual affection and charm.

Hamida's story: 'It was a girl in a mirror who started a chain of events. Shahid Hosain of Rudoli had seen, by chance, the reflection of a stunningly beautiful girl in a decorative wall mirror in a house he was visiting, and was desperate to marry her. But her parents imposed one condition: a suitable match had to be found for the younger (not so pretty) sister. Shahid Hosain talked to his good friend, Mohammed Sheikh Abdullah, who was a forty-year-old widower, and persuaded him to marry the younger sister.

This is how the two sisters Nissar Fatima and Inam Fatima of Kakori got married and came to Lucknow. Shahid and Nissar Fatima lived on 2 Mall Road, across the street from this house where Inam Fatima lived with her husband who was Taluqdar of Saidanpur which is in Barabanki district. Shahid's famous daughter, Attia Hosain has described both families and both houses in her novel, *Sunlight on a Broken Column*.

Inam Fatima belonged to a very traditional family from a small provincial town where they observed strict purdah. Her husband encouraged her to leave purdah gradually – her relations were very critical of this. She started wearing saris instead of ghararas, and accompanied her husband to parties at Government House.

WANTED

To employ for a period of five years, to be extended by mutual consent, a Eurasian lady as governess in an Oudh Taluqdar's house. Her permanent headquarters will be at 'Kasmanda', a village in Tehsil Sidhauli, district Sitapur (Oudh).

Applications to be sent to the Inspector of Schools, Lucknow, up to 15 February 1906.

The Pioneer, 18 January 1906

A series of English ladies came to live in the house to teach Inam Fatima English, and English manners and lifestyle. There was an English mania in those days and anyone with a white skin was treated as a superior person. I remember a Mrs Hyde, a good looking woman from a good family, who insisted on being served tea in her own room by the *ayah*. Most of these ladies went home before the climate got to them, selling their personal effects to add to the nest-egg of their savings.

LADY Going Home. Bust 36, W. 26, Shoes 7. Smart blue silk eve. dress, trimmed silver & lace, Rs 25. Navy & white afternoon voile dress, silk undershirt, Rs 12. Smart navy face cloth cloak, Rs 14. Green Aquasentum raincoat, Rs 45. Black & White cotton coat & skirt, Rs 6.
The Pioneer, 31 December 1914

Inam Fatima led an active and productive life till her death in 1975. This woman who had been brought up in purdah, went on to be a Member of the Legislative Assembly for 14 years – '34 to '47. She founded the school for Muslim girls, Talimgah-e-Niswah which now has 4000 students.

Inam Fatima had a daughter and three sons. When her sons were aged six, eight and nine they were sent to study at Clifton College in Brighton, England, and they did not come home for almost ten years, till the end of their schooling. Their mother saw them just once when she visited England with her husband in 1924. All the taluqdars were told by the Governor, Sir Harcourt Butler – who had become a family friend – to follow the good example set by Sheikh Abdullah and send their sons to England. It was supposed to make them pro-British – but when they saw freedom in England they wanted freedom in India.

Their youngest son Inayat, called Bubbles, had gone on to Sandhurst, and when he returned to India our mothers began matchmaking for us. He and I were allowed to become pen-friends and wrote to each other for almost a year. We got married in 1938 and led a typical army life, getting transferred from place to place, but always coming to Lucknow on visits. During the war days we used to have dinner at Kwality's and then go dancing at the Mayfair, on the roof terrace.

I entered this house 69 years ago and ever since then 11 Mall Road, or Gyara Number as we call it, has been my home.'

Sakina's story: 'My grandfather was Sir Wazir Hasan. He was the first Indian Chief Justice of the Awadh Chief Court and the title went with the job. His family was landed gentry from the Jaunpur district and he was expected to look after the estate. But he saw the opportunities that an English education would bring, quarrelled with his father and left for Aligarh University to study law.

His successful career proved him right and getting a good education became the rule in our family. His daughters (my aunts) Fatima Zehra and Noor Zehra were among the first students to get enrolled in the newly established Muslim School for Girls, later known as Karamat Hussain College. I myself have a doctorate in English Literature and taught in the same college for ten years.

My grandmother, Lady Wazir Hasan, gave up purdah in 1930, during the non-cooperation movement of Gandhiji. She gifted away all her French chiffon saris and started wearing *khadi* and weaving on a *charkha*. My mother was from Bhopal, the first girl to do a 'Middle' Exam, Class VI or Middle School. The story is that Sarojini Naidu had visited the school and mentioned my mother's looks and accomplishments to her friend Lady Wazir Hasan and that is how a proposal of marriage was put in motion.

My two brothers were enrolled as boarders in Colvin Taluqdar College and each of them had a horse and a syce. On one of their visits home they talked about the hours they spent playing *shatranj*, chess, a decadent pastime according to my mother. They were promptly transferred to Jubilee College. The daughters of lawyers, doctors, and other professionals were sent to the Girls La Martinere School, which is where I had my schooling.

My father Syyed Ali Zaheer had a law practice and a good friend of his was Justice Thomas whose sister Isabella married the Nawab of Akbarpur. They had a son who we called Tutu Nawab though his real name was Yusuf. Other contemporaries of my father's were Tej Bahadur Sapru, Gokaran Nath Misra, Bisheshwar Nath Srivastava, and Pragat Narain Mulla, father of Anand Narain Mulla. Today you will find streets in the Golagunj area, where many lawyers lived, named after all these people.

This was part of the circle of Indian friends cultivated by the Governor, Sir Harcourt Butler. He enjoyed socializing with them, wearing an Indian dress, the *angarkha*, and smoking his *pechdar* (twisted) hookah in their company.

The sons of wealthy families were sent to the *kothas*, salons of courtesans, to learn the art of civilized social behaviour from experienced tawaifs – it was the done thing. There was a category called *dereydar tawaif*, who were at the top of the hierarchy – a woman who was kept by one man and was not available to anyone else during the contracted period.

It is rumoured that a liaison between one of the family members and a tawaif called Mushtari Bai in Faizabad produced the beautiful Akhtari Bai, better known as Begum Akhtar whose unique style of singing and magnetic personality created a huge fan following.

At one point in time, Begum Akhtar's generous patron gave her a house which was right next to ours. He also gave her a huge Packard car, a gold *paandan*, beetlenut box, and a large diamond nose stud. This was some time in the early '40s.

The kotha tradition began to die out after the Zamindari Abolition Act of 1953 brought to an end the last phase of a dying culture.'

PROPOSAL

Lucknow – Friday. The women 'artists' of Chowk, who have been entertaining their admirers individually so far, may now start doing it collectively.

They are actively considering a proposal to start a 'common hall' where their admirers will be allowed on tickets and the dancers will present their programme.

The idea was put to them when a deputation of the 'artists' consisting of office-bearers of the Sangeet Kalakar Union met the local officers today.

The were told that the police would enforce the law as long as there was a suspicion that men going to the houses of the 'artists' were provided entertainment other than singing and dancing.

The Pioneer, 3 January 1959

'Nadiya Kinare' was built by Kasim Khan in the 1960s and was the only house in Lucknow with a billiard table in the basement. I relax in the large living room staring back at stuffed tiger heads. There are marvellous photographs on the wall, including one of the young Kasim Khan dressed as Lord Krishna, complete with flute. A closer inspection reveals that he is dancing on roller skates. I am welcomed by his daughter-in-law, Shamim.

Shamim's story: 'My in-laws owned the perfume factory for the manufacture of oriental perfumes which was established in 1839 by two brothers from Kannauj: Asghar Ali and Mohammed Ali. It was located in Hina Building in Chowk, which was pulled down in 2003.

The family owned a distillation plant in Gunjan in Orissa, where the *keora* plant grows. Roses came from Barwana near Aligarh, *motia*, *bela*, *chameli* and *khus* from Kannauj. When the first monsoon rain fell on clay soil, this clay was boiled in huge pots and its perfume distilled to make the aroma of rain on dry earth – *itr gil*.

When Partition happened my husband's grandfather, Haji Istifa, and some of his children decided to go to Pakistan, so 75 per cent of the family property was taken over by the Custodian. The Government allowed the children who stayed behind to keep the factory since it was their source of livelihood.

My father-in-law, Kasim Khan, was an extraordinary man, with an eagerness to live life to the full. He was always immaculately groomed and carried himself like a dancer – in his younger days he was an expert at the tango, samba, rumba, foxtrot, whatever was the rage of the moment, with whichever Anglo-Indian girl who was ready to partner him. He was a billiard player and an award-winning skater who created a sensation in the club in Mussoorie with his daring jumps and twists and other manoeuvres on roller skates. Like others of his generation, he loved *shikar* and he drove a Plymouth convertible – that was his lifestyle.'

We have just finished a typically Lucknow dinner party – everyone arriving late, spinning in from other parties. The spread on the table would be called a banquet in any other town, but here it is just an intimate dinner for 20-odd close friends, with the additional piquancy of Rampur specialities in competition with Lucknow's best cuisine. Before I leave our hostess agrees to talk to me about her memories.

I arrive at her flat the next morning. The bungalows on this lovely old road near the Lucknow Gymkhana Club have been turned into elegant apartments, just two stories high. The original ambience has not changed much.

Rana's story: 'I got married in 1964 and came from Rampur to my in-law's house which was in an old part of Lucknow, in Nakkhaas.

My husband Sarwar's ancestor was Syed Hamid Ali Khan who had the title Jalees-ud-Dowlah Bahadur. He left Shiraz in Iran and came to Lucknow where he was appointed tutor to the young Wajid Ali Shah. He continued to serve him for the rest of his life, first as tutor, then as his minister, and then as loyal follower of the nawab in exile in Matia Burj near Calcutta.

I have a document written in Persian on parchment, signed by Syed Hamid Ali Khan in the Imambara Jalees-ud-Dowlah, Matia Burj, dated 16 March 1881, declaring that the money he had spent on behalf of Nawab Wajid Ali Shah should not be reclaimed by any of his descendants.

Sometime at the end of the 19th century, one of the direct descendents came back from Matia Burj to Lucknow, even though he no longer had any close relatives here. My husband Sarwar is his grandson.

Sarwar studied in Jubilee College, as did his father before him. The men folk got employment in the colonial bureaucracy and although they gradually became westernised in their lifestyle, a breakfast of cornflakes and ovaltine rusks was accompanied by the famous Lucknow *balai*.

My mother-in-law used to observe strict purdah. Cooking was her hobby and she used to get coal *angeethis* brought into the *daalaan*, courtyard, where she lovingly prepared special dishes herself. She was fond of eating paan, and enjoyed reading Urdu novels.

I remember one woman who used to visit my mother-in-law quite frequently. She was tall and thin and her conversation was always lively and amusing. We enjoyed her company. Although she was very poor, she was treated with respect and as an equal. My mother-in-law would discretely give her gifts of clothing and money.

She was married to someone called Sanju so we called her Sanju Chachee. Sanju used to hang around the courts, pursuing various cases. He would go and collect the money for the *wazifa* that his wife was entitled to and this seemed to be their only source of income.

Sanju Chachee used to tell us fascinating stories about the time when she was married to her first husband, a nawab, and lived in a grand Mahal, with every luxury at her command: fabulous *farshi ghararas*, jewellery, a horde of servants. She herself belonged to Kanpur – during the uprising of 1857 many nawabi families of Lucknow fled to Kanpur and the area where they lived, Gwaltoli, still exists.

One day when I happened to be with her on an errand in Kashmiri Mohalla, she pointed out to me the place that had been her husband the Nawab's grand mahal. I asked her, "But why did you leave the Nawab, Chachee?"

At first she would not reply, but when I persisted she broke down and wept and told me this story.

Sanju Chachee's story: "At first I was very happy with my husband. His mother was good to me. I had every comfort. I had four sons in quick succession. Then he started to keep bad company. He used to drink and womanize all night, and return to the house at dawn. But what was worse – he got addicted to gambling. One by one he wagered and lost all our wealth, my jewellery, even parts of the house.

Early one morning the servant told me that the Rastogi jeweller wanted to see me. This was the time my husband usually returned home – I wondered what news I would get about the reason for his delay. I spoke to the jeweller from behind the curtain. Suddenly the man pulled aside the curtain and grabbed my arm. 'I won you from your husband in a betting game,' he informed me.

I screamed and ran to my mother-in-law. To this day I think the advice she gave me was the best under the circumstances. 'Put on your shoes and your burqa,' she said. 'Leave the house by the back door and never come back.'

This is what I did. I ran to the house of a relative, and from there I went to my family in Kanpur where I stayed for many years. Not once did my husband come to look for me. It was only after I heard that he had died that I came back to Lucknow. My sons were all grown up and living their own lives – they had forgotten me."

Sanju Chachee used to visit me in my home after Sarwar and I moved to our own apartment. She used to love my children and entertained them with marvellous stories. The "house" in which she lived with Sanju was nothing more than a sloping, patchwork roof erected on the side of a small yard.

In Lucknow I found that the singing of *marsiyas*, songs of mourning, during Mohurrum was the best I had ever heard. The Anjumans prepared and practiced and composed their own tunes. Naushad, the music director from Bollywood, used to come to his home town Lucknow during Mohurrum to listen to marsiyas and you can pick out these haunting melodies in some of his compositions.

My mother-in-law used to visit Afzal Mahal which was two doors away from our house and often talked about the owner, Rani Shehenshah Begum of Akbarpur, a lonely woman whose husband, only son and only grandson died in her lifetime. She herself lived till the age of a hundred, I am told. But I never saw her.'

A binding legacy

MOHAMMAD AMIR AHMAD KHAN

IT is only recently that the world has learnt that the Shia are predominant in countries other than Iran. In India they are scattered, as they tend to be in much of the world. For just under a hundred years however, Shi'ism enjoyed a unique ascendancy in Lucknow, Awadh. Once a province of the Mughal empire, its governors in the 18th century, later transformed as independent rulers, were Shia. They had once come from Iran. Burhan-ul-Mulk was appointed by the Mughal emperor as governor of Awadh. He, however, established his own court in Faizabad and assumed a manner of independence as other Mughal governors did in the wake of a tottering Mughal empire.

Under the Nawab Wazirs of Awadh, at first in Faizabad, and later in Lucknow, Shia observances achieved a unique distinction and prominence, one which embraced and influenced the entire population of Awadh. It is important to briefly appreciate the historical reasons for the various beliefs, rituals and traditions in order to better understand the culture of Shi'ism and therefore the significance of the places of congregation like the Imambaras.

One of the most important and pivotal figures in Shi'ism was Imam Hussain ibn Ali. Hussain was the Prophet's grandson and a model of piety and emulation for the Shia. His life and more importantly his martyrdom has given the Shia a distinct identity and has been one of the main influences in the evolution of the Shia and Shia thought.

It was the 10th of October 680 C.E. and also the 10th day of Muharram, the first month of the Islamic calendar, in the 61st year since the Prophet's *hijra*, or migration, from Mecca to Medina. Hussain was martyred in battle alongside all the male members of his family, barring one son who was too ill to fight. He had refused to accept Yazid's suzerainty, as doing so would have been a fundamental betrayal of the essential tenets of Islam. Yazid was the second caliph of the Umayyad dynasty and is widely acknowledged by both the Shia and Sunnis to have been a debauched, amoral tyrant. This refusal to compromise the principles of his grandfather, even in the face of profound suffering and certain annihilation, became the incomparable metaphor for truth and integrity.

Almost immediately, the news of the massacre of the Prophet's family spread throughout the region. People were aghast that such merciless treatment had been meted out to the Prophet's grandson and to his family. In Kufa, a military garrison town where the Shia population had invited Hussain to lead their revolt, people realized that they had betrayed the trust of Hussain and so in retaliation there was a surge of anti-Umayyad anger. This rebellion had a domino effect and soon revolts ignited through-out the Arabian peninsula and other Muslim lands.

While all these overtly political revolts were taking place, in Kufa and on the plains of Karbala, a small number of people collected to remember and mourn Hussain. This had far deeper and longer lasting implications than the various political movements. A group of Kufans could not bear the guilt of having betrayed the Prophet's grandson and so decided to mourn and weep for the slain family of Hussain. These people called themselves *tawwabun*, or penitents and went to

Karbala with blackened faces, dishevelled hair and torn clothes, all the while wailing in the memory of the martyrs of Karbala. The plains of Karbala became the first *Imambara*.

Azadari, or the practice of mourning the martyrdom of Hussain, in Lucknow is practiced in special halls called Imambaras and over time developed a distinctive style. A congregation at an Imambara, which follows a fairly precise procedure, is called a *majlis*. *Sozkhani* or the singing of *marsiyas* or elegies achieved an unparalleled beauty and excellence during the rule of the Nawab Wazirs of Awadh. The musical origin of sozkhani was the Hindustani classical tradition of vocal music and its concept of ragas. However, the singing was not accompanied by any instruments.

The elegies sung were poetic compositions devoted to the martyrdom of Hussain by some the finest poets that have lived in India and in Persia. Mir Anees, Mirza Dabir, Ishq, Ta'shuq are just few names. These literary masterpieces which are sung (*sozkhani*) are also declaimed (*Tahtul-lafz-khani*) from the pulpit. This unique art, whether sozkhani or Tahtul-lafz-khani (art of recitation) has virtually faded away mainly because the Urdu language has been successfully wiped out in India. Some of the Imambaras were specially built so that acoustically they supported the cantor's voice and amplified it.

The *Asafi* or Bara Imambara, the biggest *azakhana* in Lucknow, was built by Asaf-ud-Daula in 1784. It is one among countless others, big and small, in Lucknow, several of which were built by Hindus, Jhaolal's Imambara being well-known. Originally, the Asafi Imambara was commissioned because there was a devastating famine in 1783 and the Nawab wanted to provide work for people who had no other means of sustenance. According to legend, the men and women would work throughout the day and then at night the nobles, who too were affected by the famine, were called to demolish one-fourth of the structure. This was done so that work was constantly available for the poor.

The architectural style of the Asafi or Bada Imambara rivals that of some of the other great monuments, which were built by the

Mughals. Great pains were taken in order to ensure that no European style elements crept into the construction. The entrance is a triple-arched gate that leads to a sprawling garden, at the end of which is the actual building.

The main hall is an architectural marvel as it is an unsupported, un-vaulted roof, built without any stone or steel supports and is said to weigh approximately 20,000 tons. The method employed in the construction of the roof involved the use of vaults to support the weight. Only brick, rubble and mud were used and after they had set, the centring was removed. This in turn created a three dimensional labyrinth with 489 identical doorways above one of the largest unsupported roofs in Asia. The architect of the Imambara, Kifaitullah, a Persian, designed the structure so that three different halls were housed under the same roof. The China Hall is square at the ground level; it then becomes octagonal and the ceiling is 16 sided. The Persian Hall is in the middle and on the other side is the India Hall, which resembles a watermelon.

The Imambara was built in order to hold various ceremonies related to Muharram, such as the recitation of marsiyas or elegies, which are always in memory of Karbala. This is where the *ulama* or clergy delivered their sermons to crowds that could exceed 10,000. In order to ensure that everybody heard the recitations, the acoustics in the Asafi Imambara were designed so that a whisper at one end of the main hall could be clearly heard at the other. There are many legends about the Imambara. One of the most widely cited stories is that near the well complex which is a seven floored structure, the five floors that are permanently submerged under water have tunnels leading to the Gomti, the main river in Lucknow, and to Faizabad, once the seat of power of the Nawab Wazirs.

Down the road from the Bara Imambara, a descendent of Asaf-ud-Daula, Mohammad Ali Shah built a smaller Imambara. Built in 1837, its construction was also a means of providing relief and employment to the poor who had been ravaged by yet another famine. The complex also houses the tombs of Mohammad Ali Shah and his two daughters. Although the *Chota Imambara*, as the name suggests, is much smaller than its forerunner, it still has many of the original chandeliers and is an exquisite sight, especially during Muharram.

The Imambaras mentioned above are just two examples of large public azakhanas. However, most Shia houses too have some sort of Imambara, whether it is a simple cupboard, which houses a replica of the shrine of Hussain (*taziya*). Two other Imambaras which are equally famous and visited by the Shia during and after Muharram are the Imambara of Agha Baqar Sahib and Imambara of Ghufran Maab.

Every Thursday evening after sunset, hundreds of Shia and members of other denominations go to the Imambara in order to give alms to the poor and pray for the intercession of the Imams and Prophet on their behalf in order to absolve them of sins and grant them their wishes. Some Imambaras attract more people because they carry long association as places where the supplicant's wishes are granted. Other are believed to be places where miracles take place. An *Alam*, or standard of war that is now used in Muharram procession, was found in the ground over which was built Agha Baqar's Imambara. It is an especially popular site regardless of religion for both Muslims and Hindus visit it throughout the year. The Alam preserved in a special room is believed to have relieved suffering and granted wishes for well over a century

The Imambara of Ghufran Maab is situated in the Chowk area of Lucknow and is run by the descendents of Ayatollah Ghufran Maab, after whom it is named. It is one of the most popular centres of *aza* in Lucknow as it is run by the *Imam-e Juma'a*, or the leader of the congregations of Shia, in Lucknow. Traditionally, Shia Islam has always encouraged a diversity of opinions and a multiplicity of clerics in order to prevent any one person exerting undue influence. Nevertheless, there is a loose hierarchy whereby some clerics carry more weight than others. Today, Maulana Kalbe Jawad Sahib is the Imam-e Juma'a of Lucknow and looks after the Imambara of Ghufran Maab. During the first 10 days of Muharram, he reads a majlis every day to a crowd of thousands.

The Shia throughout the world will always keep the memory of Hussain alive but it is important for all Indians and not only the Shia to honour our ancestors who have left us legacies that are now often neglected and therefore disrespected. Unlike some other religious establishments, Imambaras have always been open to everyone regardless of caste, creed or religion and have never discouraged anyone from partaking in the various ceremonies. Indeed, during the months of Muharram, both Sunnis and Hindus take an active part in the processions and also openly weep in remembrance of Hussain.

Today, one often hears about various religious establishments banning the entry of the non-faithful to their houses of worship. While these views are to be respected, it is vital to acknowledge and understand that the Imambaras of Lucknow, where anyone can enter at any time, have served as a binding thread in the diverse social fabric of India. Even today they are frequented throughout the year by people of all faiths and thus serve as symbols of peace and harmony. As Indians it is our duty to help preserve these monuments which have been an integral part of Lucknow's culture for the past couple of centuries.

Shahr e Nigaaran

MUZAFFAR ALI

CULTURE is all about feeling, and it is only poets who have been able to encapsulate feelings that have been able to outlive their times and are true reflections of a culture.

Moinul Hasan Jazbi, a recent poet of Aligarh, puts across this very feeling:

Sarv o saman bhi mauj e naseeme sahar bhi hai / Ai gul tere chaman mein koi chashm tar bhi hai.

A beautiful garden abounds in tall cypress wafting in the morning breeze, birds singing, but the poet ask the flower, 'Is there anyone who feels this beauty with moist eyes?'

I thought I would give finishing touches to this piece in the garden that is Lucknow. This morning at my house in Qaiserbagh – with no trees, just a lost bulbul making a nest in a rose creeper outside my window – I am confronted by newspapers brimming with concern and misinformation about this city. There is nowhere you can go to seek the truth and knowledge about this dying civilization.

The Lucknow Times stares at you with an article titled, 'The Fine Art of Neglect'. It talks of Lucknow as a city of nawabs, not realizing that for the last 150 years there has been no nawab in the Awadh and during these years, culture, or whatever was left of it, has been nursed by its taluqdars. Mohammad Ali Shah is wrongly referred to as Mahmud Ali Shah. As one turns the pages one finds Kalbe Sadiq, one of the city's most important pillars of learning, referred to as Kalbe Siddiqui, and there is mention of Muzaffar Ali's lesser known film 'Chilman', which incidentally he never made.

Today we are a media-fed nation, nursed on misinformation and misplaced concerns. It is therefore all the more important to feel things deeply and reflect internally if one wishes to create a protective warmth around cultures. This can only be done through films, because we from Lucknow belong to a civilization of a dead language, Urdu.

> Hai khayal e mahfile dostan kisi ajnabi ka hai ye bayan / Vo jahan
> na samjhe meri zabaan vahi qismaton se mila vatan

…bemoans the Urdu poet Raghupati Sahai Firaq Gorakhpuri.

> In a congregation of friends,
> even the aliens feel,
> where none understand my language
> is destined to be my land.

I now feel at a loss as to who can enrich me with this culture. Those who know even a little have either an agenda or are arrogant. The free flowing expression of feelings which I experienced even a decade back, are no more. And it was this very fear of losing footprints of time that made me make the films that I did.

For me film-making is a means to an end, the end being a balance of the human situation with aesthetics. This balance has always been disturbed when any form of exploitation sets in, be it social, cultural or economic.

Being rooted in a continuously evolving human situation is a never ending source of renewal of a creative force. This creative surge inwardly connects all art forms. For me as an artist, Awadh is the centre of my creative chemistry. Even if I work in other cultures or languages, the grace of Awadh stands me in good stead.

Lucknow for me was a vast expanse of Awadhian landscape as you entered and left the city, changing hues in different seasons and times of the day. It was no big city in which I grew up. You could enter from one end and come out at the other within 10 or 15 minutes. This expansive Awadhian landscape opened up through avenues of giant trees, many over 200 years old. Today, for as much as an hour, there are none as you drive out of the city into the countryside. Trees within the city too have been chopped off, save in a few pockets here and there. Memories of the changing moods of nature have suddenly gone dry, with not even photographs to celebrate the past. These years that went into the making of our minds and feelings – the sense of silence, the spatial experience of the eyes – have all vanished. Ancient cultures invariably placed great emphasis on the importance of space to our well-being – and neglecting it seems to have led to confusion, conflict and general negativity in our modern society. Empty space began to irk uncivilized people, and so did silence.

Today, bodies are strewn all over the footpaths, hanging in awkward positions from rickshaws. Lucknow has lost its relationship with civilization and nature. Possibly the gory sight of bodies of Indians hanging from trees following the siege of Lucknow in 1857 has made people indifferent to these magnificent trees.

And from then on Lucknow was a birthplace of a new kind of poetry – the poetry of separation of Radha from her lover. What Wajid Ali Shah wrote as he was being exiled from his land of dreams remains unparalleled in the history of emotions:

dar o deewar pe hasrat se nazar karte hain
khush raho ahle watan ham to safar karte hain
hamne apne dile nazuk to jafa ko saunpa
Qaisari bagh jo hai usko saba ko saunpa.

Slowly this too was silenced; there were no listeners, no moaners; a new and deadly city was born as the old city was left to die a painful death. To date the beautiful old city of Lucknow with its narrow streets reels in filth and squalor, devoid even of any sewer lines to clean its gutters. The new colonial rulers avoided all contact with people of the old city and the people of the old city kept away from the language of their oppressors, thus leaving this wonderful city and its people way behind in the race for existence.

Over the years the same language that killed a culture has become the global *lingua franca*. Even as its knowledge helps unearth the many atrocities committed in 1857, it has become a challenge to understand Persian, Arabic and even Urdu. Yet, we are nowhere near the signs of bringing the past back to life. There are complex issues to be addressed. Maybe some grassroot films with a popular base can resuscitate pride, restore our lost dignity and values, which ironically have become a victim to mindless Hindi cinema. Another sad prey of this mindlessness is the beauty of silence in which you could once hear birds calling to share the beauty of its garden.

Cultures as we would like to feel them will survive when we grow out of magnified visual ugliness and horrific amplified sounds. Cultures speak to the heart and any imposition through amplified sound as in modern India is a sure way of ringing in their death knell. Hindi films, Indian politics and religion are solely responsible for this mindless assault on our sensibility and whatever that remains of our acquired refinement. This is the curse of a free and modern India, an India fragmented into a new economic classification, which has no visible meeting point. How then can we expect any concern or feeling to emerge amongst people in this newly formed social order. Lucknow, like every other city of this country, is a victim of this malaise. Unfortunately, in the case of Lucknow there is a lot more to loose.

> *Vahshat ne vo bhi loot li dam bhar mein dosto*
> *Jo muddaton mein ayi thi shaistagi hamein.*
>
> In a moment all was lost at the hands of insanity, the refinement acquired over centuries of evolution.

Beyond the magnificence of the Awadhian landscape, its unique Indo-Persian, European architecture, its very evolved gastronomic recipes, is the beauty of the language. Despite the external onslaught it remained preserved in the veils of the most exquisite feminine feudal culture the world has ever known, to the extent that even the male poets were drawn to writing in the feminine gender – a poetic form known as *rekhti*.

For me poetry became a way of feeling people and their times. It was a mother art, of expressing childhood fantasies, adventure and chivalry, valour and romance, sensuality and love, love and surrender. Poetry was a double-edged sword. It also killed the poet with the misplaced values and wrongly intentioned objectives. Fortunately, the poets of Awadh were wounded and passionate, therefore Awadh remained alive. These poets were rooted, earthy, sophisticated and spiritual.

Lucknow has been the city of both the written and spoken word – the language of day to day life, of humour and etiquette, of love and romance, of poetry and eulogy. Even the unlettered wrote poetry and spoke in velvet smooth tones. Today the city is confronted with cinema and television, with the language of politics and modern education. Political bigwigs from outside Awadh have devastated the delicate and vulnerable ethos of this city that has given its identity.

There was a time and place where everything beautiful came without any cost, like the wind and water, where art was created with passion, with an urge to share without commercial compensation, when people created a warmth and excitement for each other with everything within their means. Today people are helpless and alienated.

> *Taveel hone lagi hain isi liye ratein*
> *Ki log sunte sunate nahin kahin bhi.*

The poet Shahryar bemoans the length of endless nights, for no one tells stories any more. Lucknow was a centre of this art form, *Daastaan Goi*, and modern Aligarh, as I knew it, was a centre for reflecting on concerns for the evolution of a mindless modern India, devoid of any feelings, contributing to the loss of a language which evolved with great sophistication in Lucknow.

The world of story telling in poetic form that engulfs the mind, heart and soul is the *Masnavi*. Be it in the realm of chivalry and martial arts as in the *Shahnameh* of Firdausi, or a spiritual unfolding as in the Masnavi of Maulana Jalaluddin Rumi, or Khusrau or Nizami. The first Masnavi in Urdu was written by Mir Hasan – *Benazir o Badr e Munir*, soon followed by Pandit Daya Shankar Nasim's *Gulzar e Nasim*, Mirza Shauq's *Bahar e Ishq* and, *Zahr e Ishq* and *Fareb e Ishq*. The Masnavi was the equivalent of the world of moving images of today. Contemporary moving images have little to do with creating an active imagination while the Masnavi made people own and posses it, depending on their power to remember and recite or even through feeling with their heart. Zahr e Ishq was prohibited because of the kind of effect it had on young lovers. It is said that many committed suicide consumed by the passion and helplessness of the lovers in the Masnavi.

The *marsiya* was a form of recreating events with deep feelings that would move the audience to tears. Its poets had reached the pinnacle of their art form in making audiences emotionally charged. The martyrdom of Imam Hussain, the grandson of the Prophet of Islam in the battle of Karbala, was the only subject of this sacred art form which prospered in the reign of the Awadh rulers who emanated from Khorasan and belonged to the Shia faith.

Mir Anis and Mirza Dabir took this art form to heights which cut across all boundaries of faith and religion, and as fate may have it, divided the city into followers or lovers of either Mir Anis or Mirza Dabir. Anis made recitation into an art form, known as *marsiya khwani*. With change of expression, with an underlining of a gesture, using the highs and lows of a human voice he could touch and rip the heart apart.

David Mathew in translating the marsiyas of Mir Anis says of the Urdu language, 'Urdu is an Indian language which while readily absorbing grammatical structures and vocabulary from Arabic and Persian, possesses a vast number of synonyms. For words like "horse", "sword", "battle", "desert", etc., which naturally frequent the marsiya, more than half a dozen Urdu words might be found for each, and of course, they will be used by the poet wishing to display his linguistic virtuosity. English though a rich language, is in comparison often found wanting. This presents a great problem to the translator, who must make the best of what he has at his disposal.'

> Enough, Anis! Your very limbs are quaking.
> This monument you built with glory rings.

> Such verses written while your hands were shaking / will fire the world and please the hearts of kings.

> Their harvest is this gathering of mourning
> the spring-like pleasure of autumn's dawning.

It is only from a deep realization you find something you have lost. This is the only ray of hope on the firmament of the twilight of Awadh.

Cultures take centuries to evolve, but fade away faster than we think. Lucknow has been sighing for over a century and a half, but somehow it is only recently that modern communication and tourism has begun to question its sad state, through which nostalgia has begun to emerge larger than life, as a saviour of this fabled region.

The first war of independence in 1857, termed as a mutiny by the colonial rulers, and then independence designed to be coupled with the partition, subsequently leading to a communal resurgence followed by sharp caste division in politics, has left Lucknow bruised and battered.

But Lucknow has not left the gaze of those who think with the heart. Commentaries on its plight have found expression in words of modern poets though they may not belong to Lucknow. Shahryar wrote these words in the aftermath of the breaking of the Babri Mosque in 1993:

> *Har khawab ke makan ko mismaar kar diya hai / behtar dinon ka aana dushwaar kar diya hai.*

> Every abode of dreams has been shattered
> The coming of better days made increasingly difficult.

The biggest loss came from the partition – a deep and silent loss which still echoes in the large vaulted roof of the Bara Imambara, in the slum-like but once grand palace of Qaiserbagh, the largest quadrangle in Asia. The big question that haunted my father, and I have inherited this concern, is how prominent Muslim taluqdars could ever dream of an integrated Awadh in a nation divided along communal lines. Did they think they would slice off their heritage and transplant it across the border? And whatever happened is the saddest moment in the history of civilization of the subcontinent.

Ever since, the cancer of communalism has continued to spread on this sacred soil of legends, masnavis, marsiyas and *ghazals*. The very basis of the existence of our culture has been hacked off; the language – Urdu, the language of the heart, the language of love, the language of the soul, of imagination, humour and wit. This innocent language began to be associated with the cause of the partition, of a community and those taluqdars who became its icons and flag bearers. When we will emerge out this darkness is hard to say.

A modern poet of Aligarh, Rahi Masoom Raza, comes to our rescue and exhorts us:

> *Kisi shokh shola ru koi intekhab lao*
> *Shab e gham guzarni hai koi aftab lao*
> *kisi chehre kitabi ka sunao koi kissa*
> *vahi lahjae tammana vahi aab o taab lao*
> *ye chiragh jaise lamhe yuhin raegaan ne jaen*
> *koi khaab dekh daalo koi inquilab lao.*
> Bring a match for that coquettish flaming face
> bring the sun to the dark nights of despair.
> Tell a story of a beauty found in books
> bring the same endearing tone and lustre fair.
> Don't let these flickering moments go
> Dream, and bring a change in the air.

As a filmmaker and as an artist I have begun to explore the process of reality and realization, history and reflection, current affairs and inferences. Lucknow is one such situation which needs reading between lines and motivating people to take certain positions which can retrieve the damage. It can only happen if one aims at the heart and focuses on grassroot grievances and their causes.

Poets, soldiers, saints and kings, Awadh has seen them take birth on its sacred soil, surviving vested interests and political upheavals, surfacing over and over again, and remaining alive in the hearts of their people. The Sufi way is the way of becoming invisible; of not knowing and being ignorant; of receiving and giving – the way of a woman; the way of Umrao Jaan, the way of saying and feeling and not being a burden.

The beauty of Awadh is that it expanded its arms to take everything heart-rending into its fold. The exploits and adventures of Lord Krishna were expressed in an operatic art form of the *Rahas*. Faiths were bridged when the nawab, Wajid Ali Shah, wrote and danced as Lord Krishna or a lovelorn yogi. He opened the gates of his Qaiserbagh palace with fairs and festivals and *sabhas*. Mian Amanat, a contemporary of Wajid Ali Shah, wrote the *Indar Sabha*.

Poets are the mirrors of society. They are dreamers of an ideal world, the romantics that bring about change. Unfortunately, the poets of Lucknow have been more subtle and laid back. As Mohammad Iqbal says, 'Nations are born in the hearts of poets and die in the hands of politicians.' There was no Faiz or Makhdoom or Iqbal to stir the passion for revolt, but the silent marsiya of the city has acquired the power of a huge emotional upsurge which can change the world.

awwal shab vo bazm ki raunaq shamma bhi thi parwana bhi / raat aakhir hote hote hote khatm tha yeh afsana bhi

daur e massarat Aarzoo apna itna zalzala aageen tha / hath se muhn tak aate aate choot chala paimana bhi.

– Aarzoo Lakhnavi

Thus Lucknow continues to live on in two ways; one through its past, and the other through a sensitive and creative reflection of what it has been through. Artists have expressed and continue to express all that Lucknow has been through in the past, the recent and not so recent. On the other hand, scholars who attempt to place Awadh in its right dialectical predicament, can only identify areas of exploitation and point out the imbalance in the human situation and take stock of ugliness – some reversible some irreversible, like the ancient chopped trees and communalized brains.

The biggest and most silent power that empowers Awadh today and creates a softness of the heart is none other than Haji Waris Ali Shah, the Sufi saint of the Chishti order who passed away in 1905.

His inspiration has kept alive the poetry of the soul through poets like Bedam Shah Warsi and the entire genre of *qawwali* singing in Awadh. Who has as many Hindu disciples as Muslims. It is truly through this spiritual connection that the *Ganga Jamuni tehzeeb* (culture) is kept alive.

My Lucknow

SALEEM KIDWAI

I LEFT Lucknow in 1968 to go to college in Delhi, believing that I was severing my connection with the city. I used to return regularly for vacations but gradually the visits became briefer and seemed to coincide mostly with weddings or funerals which, given that I was a part of multiple extended families, were many. I saw little of the city and had no friends in it except those who lived in Delhi like me. What struck me on these visits was the rot, not decay.

I returned 35 years later to live here again in the town I was born, but not in my old home, hoping that this address would now never change. Delhi had become home, but an increasingly uncomfortable one. Mercifully, there was another home from which my umbilical cord had never been completely severed.

The year I left, the state of Uttar Pradesh was under President's rule for the first time in its history. Charan Singh, a former Congressman, had breached the hold of the INC, but lasted as chief minister for only a year. When I returned, Mayawati was midway between her 18 month long third stint as chief minister. The first had lasted four months and the second six.

When I returned to Lucknow towards the end of 2002, her second partnership with the BJP was in increasing trouble. Soon thereafter, she chose to demonstrate her electoral might by calling one of her massive rallies which was organized by the low profile cadre of her party. I had never seen such a large demonstration in Lucknow. It changed the look of the city. Apart from the abundance of posters, wall graffiti, flags and cutouts, there was, floating above the black phallic structure that emerged from the centre of Parivartan Chowk, a large, blue, plastic inflatable elephant hovering proudly in the skyline alongside the marvellous domes of two nawabi tombs.

This Chowk was important to Mayawati. She had casually ignored protest from conservationists and the heritage zone laws to create a gallery of Dalit icons at one of the city's busiest roundabouts in Hazratganj. Soon the seams of the elephant, like those of her alliance, began to come apart and as the helium leaked, the blue blimp started contorting into bizarre shapes as it descended against the setting sun. By evening the elephant was breathing its last on the ground, a crumpled plastic sheet. The next morning it was up again, gaily floating, plastic blue against the blue of the sky. Politics in UP did appear somewhat like a circus with its trapeze artists, tightrope walkers, musclemen, clowns and, of course, elephants.

Our old home in Lucknow had been a busy and a crowded one. Relatives frequently came to visit and others to live with us in order to go to school or college. These were cousins from the neighbouring district of Barabanki whose parents watched over the inheritance of our extended family — homes, lands and orchards. Male cousins usually headed for Aligarh, but for the female cousins, Lucknow was the obvious and convenient choice. They had a wide selection of options – Karamat Hussain Muslim Girls College, Mahila Vidyalaya, Bharti Balika Vidyalaya, Loreto Convent, St. Agnes School or the Isabella Thoburn College. They stayed away from Lucknow University, mostly because it had co-education.

Today, almost no one is left in the family homes in Barabanki. And none of the younger relatives, male or female, want to stay on in Lucknow to study if they can help it. Aligarh too is no longer considered the only other option, which now includes the US, Canada, Australia and even New Zealand.

We used to live on the edge of Hazratganj. I knew where to get what I needed. I could walk to six of the best movie halls and the other three were an easy *rikhshaw* or bicycle ride away. The British Council library was less than a 10 minute walk. I had gotten membership without sponsors or a deposit by simply filling a form and showing my school identity card. The American Information Centre was a bit further. In the same building as the BCL were two of my favourite haunts – the Mayfair Cinema and Ram Advani Booksellers. Also in the same building was a place I would have loved to go more often, the Kwality restaurant famous for its ice creams and pastries, the fanciest restaurant of the time. I distinctly remember my first impressions of the place – regular, discreet tip tap of cutlery hitting china and the discreet hum of genteel conversation.

Across the road was the almost as posh Royal Café. The libraries and the cinema halls were once the only places I spent time in which were air conditioned. Close by was Ranjana Café where I must have had my first hundred odd dosas. Ranjana has been replaced by Barista. Royal Café has moved location but has an elaborate *chat* stall outside its entrance and serves most of its patrons on the sidewalk. I rarely went to the legendary Indian Coffee House at one end of Hazratganj which also has a chat stall at its entrance. Kwality, Mayfair and the British and American libraries have gone. The only survivor is the bookshop and Ram Advani continues to zealously interact with anyone interested in books.

My family was religious but religion was confined to the home. I never had a close friend who was Muslim. My father had numerous close friends who were not Muslims. I don't ever recall them discussing their own or the others' religion. Special care was taken never to be disrespectful to anyone's sensitivities. The issue of his friends' religions seemed to only come up after my father's return from *shikar* in the winters when the loot of beautiful dead birds had to be distributed. His bag was usually overflowing, often consisting of over 50 visitors from Siberia. They were sorted out to see which were *halal*. The birds were shot from a boat which was then rowed out to pick up the prey felled in the sky. Immediately they had to be killed in the Islamic way, which meant running a knife under their gullet while declaring one's faith. If blood flowed from the artery of the dying bird, it was considered kosher. If the bird was already dead, many non-Muslims would be happy to have it.

This did change though as the size of the bag shrank and there was less and less game to be given away. A friendly maulvi gave the *fatwa* that if the necessary utterances had been made at the moment of pulling the trigger, the birds were halal. I haven't eaten duck killed in shikar since I left Lucknow.

We always lived surrounded by non-Muslims. If we referred to neighbours in generic terms, it was as Bengali, Punjabi, Madrasi, Kashmiri and so on and, in the case of Christians, as *Angrez* (if they were fair) and Anglo-Indians if they were not. I learnt much later that one of my father's close friends was Jewish. This was a revelation for he was the only Indian Jew that I have known. I asked my mother why she had not told me this. 'What was there to tell?' she answered. I try and recall any Hindu-Muslim divide in my world then, but fail to.

Things seemed to change drastically in the middle years of my absence. I remember suddenly feeling afraid of travelling on the Lucknow Mail, boxed in close to belligerent groups of saffron bandana anointed *kar sevaks*. Their threat was palpable and one tried to become invisible. Some relatives made train reservations using Hindu names and a female relative wore a *bindi* for extra protection. I learnt not to react when referred to as *Babar ki Aulad*, but despaired at how the heritage of Lucknow was not just being shredded but also mocked, how the idea of Awadh had to be destroyed before a political party could rule India. Today, I can't help but contrast that feeling of fear with the overt assertion of identity when I see an increasing number of people across the city who can be recognized as being Muslim from the way they dress.

I remembered pilgrims on the Grand Trunk Road between Lucknow and Barabanki that leads to Ayodhya. These pilgrims were doing arduous physical penance – carrying sacred water over long distances or measuring this distance with their bare bodies. There were lot more pilgrims on the route during the anti-Babri Masjid agitation but they were in open trucks screaming at the top of their voices. No piety was visible in these new pilgrims, only hate.

If I remember any religious wariness in my initial life in Lucknow, it was between the Sunnis and the Shias. If there was 'the other', then the Shias came closest to it. The religious education given at home had a disproportionate amount of history compared to belief, doctrine or ritual. And the history naturally was a partisan one. Suspicions ran deep. I remember the lady who looked after me when I was a child, repeatedly telling me to never eat or drink anything offered by a Shia, 'for,' she said, 'they spit in what they offer you.' Nearly 50 years later I heard of the reaction of an elderly Shia lady about the marriage of her nephew to a Hindu. 'He is married and that is all that matters to me. And then, at least he didn't marry a Sunni.' Yet I am sure I never heard anyone argue that Shias should stop being Shias or that they needed to change.

I now live in Mahanagar, across the Gomti from Hazratganj. Mahanagar was the first ambitious urban colonization undertaken by the government after independence. As kids when we passed Mahanagar on our frequent trips to our parents' homes in Barabanki, we believed we were out of Lucknow for soon there were fields and mango orchards on either side of the highway which was an endless tunnel under branches of huge trees. Today, there are buildings and institutions all the way from Lucknow to Barabanki city, 25 kilometres away. The last of the magnificent trees have been recently bulldozed and lie as deadwood waiting to be removed. You never get the feeling you have left the city.

Again, I find myself living in the middle of the city although the city seems a hundred times larger. New Lucknow has mushroomed all around me. Derivative and glitzy, it is not the city I knew. I am often rudely reminded of how it has changed but soon enough I'm reassured that in many ways it hasn't and that one better be grateful for it. There is the lilt of the language and the polite phrases one begins to hear when one boards the Shatabdi. Lucknow is still a city where people prefer to be polite and courteous and don't believe that rudeness is the best way to get things done.

When we were searching for a new home, our preference for Mahanagar was often discouraged. The attraction of Mahanagar was that the houses resembled those that Lucknow had when I was growing up. It's a BJP colony, we were told and that was a brief jolt. Having been shown houses where marble paving in open spaces ensured that not even a blade of grass could grow through the cracks, a split-level living room with a waterfall, a house where the bathroom, with its jacuzzi, was bigger than the living room or any of the bedrooms, and one with a waterbed with a large headboard shaped like a butterfly, I wasn't going to let a political party decide where I chose to live.

On moving in, it was heartening to discover that the *mohalla* spirit was still alive and word had already spread in the streets around. First-time visitors who asked for help were usually directed correctly. What was disheartening was that the good samaritans always wanted to know if it was the Muslims who had just moved in that they were looking for.

The local BJP municipal corporator often says the most communal things when invited to the Residents Welfare Association meetings. Complaints to other members engenders awkwardness; they invariably apologize on her behalf and assure us that they don't agree with her. They also request us not to make a fuss because she would be useful if the colony is ever to get some basic civic facilities like a sewer. Again the dilemma is easy to resolve, for in this city neighbours are more important than political parties.

The city has many claimants for both its past and its future. The Sahara group was clearly the first off the mark in introducing the fruits of globalization to the city. They staked their claim to the city by trying to make Sahara synonymous with Lucknow in their advertizing campaigns. If their hoardings were to be believed, one had arrived in Sahara city when one arrived at Amausi airport. Sahara city is actually a 'fortress like' city the group has built on the edge of Lucknow, very much in the tradition of medieval military usurpers. Inside it, people are decreed to greet each other with a salute in the name of Sahara.

Across the rest of the city the Sahara group has made its presence felt by altering the skyline. They built their mall, Sahara Ganj, the first in Lucknow, next door to Hazratganj. Sahara Ganj, bathed in mauve light, instantly became a popular tourist site. Forget that the new attraction came at the heavy cost of amputating one of the wings of the charming Carlton Hotel. Page Three projected the Roys as the first family of the city. The new nawabs of Lucknow also gave the city its first internationally noticed celebrity wedding. Its organization and cost would easily have matched any of the nawabi extravaganzas.

Then there are those citizens who see their future in protesting the loss of heritage, of course, conceived of as only nawabi. They market nawabdom as if it was a fragile antique and believe in lament, the time-honoured way to deal with loss. I remember a mock public funeral procession for the death of the culture of Lucknow in which mourners, some theatrically dressed, walked behind a mock bier representing the city's heritage. It was a photo-op for a starved press, not a political statement. The octogenarian Hamida Habibullah was among the mourners and for those who cared to notice, visibly embarrassed. Later she admitted to having come because she believed it had something to do with conservation. She saw what was going on, but as a true Lakhnavi was far too gracious to leave immediately.

They ranted to the press during the run-up to the release of the new *Umrao Jaan*, irate that J.P. Dutta had insulted Lucknow with the many misrepresentations in his film, without of course having seeing it. The turbans were all wrong for they were Rajasthani rather than nawabi, as were the costumes. The worst blasphemy was Dutta saying that he had not shot in Lucknow because the city's monuments were

so badly maintained. Dutta would have to apologize for saying this,
they threatened, before they would let the film be shown in Lucknow.
Not once did it strike them or the journalists, as to why they were
protesting at something that they had themselves routinely cried
hoarse over. After all, did they too not maintain that the monuments
of Lucknow had been allowed to go to seed? Once the film was
released the criticism changed. The refrain then became how much
better and more authentic the *Umrao Jaan* made by *hamare* Muzaffar
Ali was.

The *hijab* wearing Begums of Lucknow (read Awadh) too rose
to the defence of 'our Umrao'. At a press conference they raved about
how Umrao had been misrepresented or insulted in the film. This
could have been a ground-breaking effort to raise issues around gender
representation or indeed of the *tawaif*. However, it didn't seem as if
any of the spokespersons had even read the novel, and if so, had paid
attention while reading. What most upset them were scenes of Umrao
in a swimming pool, and a tiled one at that! The delicious irony of the
Begums fighting for the reputation of a tawaif was lost on all.

Soon after I returned to Lucknow, I spoke at the opening session
of an all India teacher's conference at the university about same sex
love. It was a learning experience for me. Apart from the wide eyes
in the audience, the hostility was muted, the positions on the issue
politically correct, even if token. After the conference I met nearly a
dozen people who wanted to speak to me, one to one. These were
research scholars, women and men who had already written but
not published on the subject. What blew my mind was that their
exclusive interest, intellectual and otherwise, was centred on lesbians.
Lucknow is a city which has seen two of the most outrageous police
actions against homosexuals in the last six years. Evidently, the earlier
notion of Lucknow as the home of nawabi *shauq* for *laundas* needs to
be revisited.

These five years have been fascinating and enraging. They cover
the fall and rise of Mayawati, and the surreal tenure of the Mulayam
Singh government. That Mayawati was clearly to be the most
influential political figure in the region was apparent.

Living under Mayawati's 'rule', certain things became clear immediately. Ambition was a finely honed instinct. She was strong-willed, self-made and convinced of her destiny. She paid attention to criticism only if it meant a loss of votes. She wanted to rule the state as she did her party, by herself with help of hand-picked aides, not leaders with their own base. She had a ruler's penchant for monumental architecture in stone, laying gardens surprisingly bereft of trees and for planting large statues of people whose legacy she had decided to tap. She also commissioned her own statue to stand alongside that of Ambedkar and Kanshi Ram. She governed as rulers of yesteryears did.

Senior civil servants who dropped in to buy books at Ram Advani Booksellers often stayed on to chat. Some shook their heads in disbelief as they talked of her irreverent attitude towards bureaucrats, her disdain for complicated administrative rules in an eagerness to find shortcuts around them, her unacceptable hurry to get things done. Others in the Muhammad Bagh Club, their tongues loosened by long stints in the bar, focused on gender and caste to rubbish her. One exceptionally indiscreet remark stands out: 'Remember what happened to Phoolan Devi? No woman gets away with insulting a thakur.'

The last comment was made after Mayawati had taken on Raja Bhaiyya, the influential politician. By imprisoning him and his father, she sent a message across the caste spectrum that she wasn't going to be cowed down, thereby outraging many thakurs in the state. Moreover, by welcoming D.P. Yadav (a don) into her party, she made it clear that she was ready to take them on. We too have our own *bahubalis* she had proclaimed. She even campaigned for Narendra Modi while in alliance with the BJP.

But the lady, a true politician, knows the advantages of makeovers. She dented Mulayam's Muslim vote bank and the BJP's upper caste one, the same that her party's cadre had earlier demanded be publicly thrashed with shoes. Reportedly, she is now ordering a makeover of even her statues.

Many in Lucknow were happy to see her go because they were tired of her shenanigans, her penchant for constantly being in the headlines of the newspapers and TV. There was a lot of talk about Mayawati and her diamonds. She had publicly flashed them for all to see. As for those reportedly gifted to her, a loyal bureaucrat tried to explain after she had resigned: 'She is innocent, childlike (*masoom*). She believes that the pieces of glass that people give her are diamonds.'

I must confess that I had welcomed the return of Mulayam the Lohiaite, the most articulate spokesman for secularism in UP. I also welcomed one of his first announcements, that student elections would be allowed again and that they would be held as soon as possible. It, however, didn't take long to see why they had been banned in the first place. Student leaders appeared to be political goons, totally unconcerned with academic issues because they were not in the university to attend lectures. The only academic matter that concerned Mulayam and over which he was even ready to precipitate a constitutional showdown was the creation of another liberally funded government university, one to be headed by a political crony. This was the university meant to teach Persian and Arabic in Rampur. It was difficult to decide whether to weep or laugh for the Persian department of the Lucknow University no longer had students, and the department survived only because the Maharaja of Kapurthala who had endowed the university with land had made it a condition that the university would always have a Persian department.

Mulayam Singh's tenure as CM seemed like a farce scripted by a Bollywood hack. The Lohiaite suddenly turned into a CEO of a brand with an non-constitutional MD, a brand ambassador and so on. The slogan chosen was that the state had suddenly become an *Uttam* Pradesh. The government organized events with glitterati, mostly from Bombay films, and their groupies on the dais, our 'Sahara' Roy among them. Anil Ambani was projected as the one leading the state into industrialization and riches. Amitabh Bachchan served as its brand ambassador and his family was willing to appear when asked to tell the people how lucky they were to be living under Samajwadi rule. His wife was appointed to various official bodies and the Rajya Sabha. Films starring the Bachchans were given tax exemption. In his eagerness Mulayam, the vocal critic of dynasty, even insulted his own brand ambassador by giving the little B the highest government honour which only recently had been bestowed first on Harivansh Rai Bachchan and then on the big B.

Soon political scandal went beyond graft and become underground sleaze. As law and order deteriorated, there was nostalgia for Mayawati because she got 'things done'. 'She never bothered about hierarchy,' a police officer recalled. 'If there was trouble, she herself called the remotest of *thanas* and gave orders.'

Now that I think of it, a bureaucrat had said that she would come back with an independent majority if only she could manage the Muslim votes. That she clearly did and if she can consolidate her current constituency, she will almost certainly become a political player, and not just in UP. Lucknow will be a good place to watch these developments. Mayawati already seems a changed politician, and in the possibilities of a makeover lies hope.

Destined for mediocrity

YUSUF ANSARI

'Lamentation was raised in the realm. Day by day, the people were being looted. No one listened to their complaints. All the wealth of the countryside was being drawn into Lucknow and squandered on prostitutes, jesters, and other kinds of vilasita (decadence). Day by day the debt to the English Company kept growing. Day by day the blanket grew wetter and felt heavier. Because there was no proper administration in the country, even the annual revenue was not received. The [British] resident repeatedly gave warnings, but people here were besotted with the drunkenness of vilasita; no one had the least idea what was happening.'

Shatranj ke Khiladi (The Chess Players)
by Premchand. First published in 1924.

LIKE its literary symbol, Ruswa's Umrao Jaan – the much chronicled (and courted) courtesan – modern Lucknow exists as perspective. These range from a lost Venice of the Orient for Romanticists pining to find some glamorous reference to recent North Indian history, to a doomed Babel for anthropologists tracking the weighty matter of urban planning and development (or lack of it) in modern India. Alternatively, it becomes a New World beckoning parochial parvenus in search of their share of India's 'new economy' or a 'second paradise on earth' for members of a new triangular elite representing the working nexus of crime, politics and commerce.

The 'indigenous' culture of Lucknow was historically destined for exactly the kind of state it is in. The city of Lucknow and the larger *tehzeeb* and *adab* of Awadh that we hear so much of today as a nostalgic poser, were merely a repository for the declining values of one power (the Mughals in Delhi), and an expectant recipient of another empire (the British in Calcutta). In such a circumstance, Lucknow was already speeding towards a crisis of identity. Even as the capital of Uttar Pradesh, Lucknow can no longer exhibit a culture of its own, such as Benaras, never severed from its ancient religious roots can, or Kanpur, unashamedly and convincingly commercial and industrial does.

The dismantling of 'Old Lucknow' began with the partition of the subcontinent in 1947. However, the traditional hypothesis that partition was singularly responsible for the decline of Lucknow, as a city of intangibles such as 'high culture', learning and social grace, cannot form a basis for any scientific inquiry into its urban decline. The period between 1947 and 1987 was a sterile interlude in the city's existence. No major architectural innovations were added to its skyline; nor was it at the centre of any significant movement whether literary, political or of any other kind. Certainly, no economic 'boom' came its way and Lucknow did not become a point of reference for India's New Economy such has its counterpart in the Deccan, Hyderabad.

There is much between the two cities that merits comparison. Break-away factions of the imperial Mughal court founded both cities in the 18th century. Both were ruled by rulers belonging to minority communities (Muslim), ruling over subjects belonging to majority communities (Hindu). Both cities witnessed social violence in the aftermath of the partition of India, Hyderabad significantly more so in 1949 with its accession to the Union of India. Yet, 60 years after independence both the method and measure of how the two cities have developed cannot be starker.

It is not a tradition of political activism that keeps Lucknow alive in the national mind. The cause for Lucknow's continuity as a city of any significance was and continues to be its political *location*. As the capital of Uttar Pradesh (which alone accounts for almost 15% of the total seats in Parliament), it is the seat of administration for India's most populous state with the largest state assembly in the country. The social complexities of Uttar Pradesh, whose caste demographics reveal an almost even proportion of upper-caste Hindus, Muslims, Scheduled Castes and Other Backward Castes, make it a political (though not cultural) melting pot. If we look at two political movements, which symbolized national politics in the last decade – the Mandal agitation and the Ram Janmabhoomi/Babri Masjid movement – it is notable that neither of these located themselves in Lucknow and nor did they use the city as a centre, though they were centred in North India. Yet, the political activism of a large section of the leadership central to the mobilization of both these agitations had their roots in Lucknow.

Indeed the former BJP Prime Minister A.B. Vajpayee represents the Lucknow seat in the Lok Sabha. Mulayam Singh Yadav, Mayawati and Kalyan Singh are names that are synonymous with the political culture of Uttar Pradesh and, therefore, the political economy of Lucknow. Their protégés, some of whom are Members of the Legislative Assembly (MLA's), serve the dual purpose of filling up seats in the state assembly and managing the commercial interests of their respective bosses. In an urban environment where the commercial interests of senior politicians can only be safeguarded by criminal methods, law enforcement becomes peripheral if not obsolete. A self-pitying shield of nostalgia and motley bundles of recollections that represent the collective values of the elite of 'old Lucknow' are an inadequate protection against the highly motivated industry of ruthless self-preservation being run by the operators of its new political economy. Protest, opposition and any prospects of confrontation against the new order seem unlikely.

The situation of those who lament the new order is not unlike that of the former aristocracy of Awadh who, 'Unable to withstand the pressure of changing times, the later nawabs of Awadh turned inwards. They sequestered themselves in a realm of their own imagining, behind walls, behind the gaze of the invader. Here, they invented a world of fantasy – with its own language, logic and meaning...There was no place for such a vision in the age of the Industrial Revolution, and the brutal world of international power politics.'[1]

The only difference for them is that the Industrial Revolution has been substituted by caste devolution, and the 'brutal world of international power politics' has been replaced by the worst aspects of parochialism. What remains of 'Old Lucknow' exists only as symbol or metaphor. Therefore, while the building that houses the Legislative Assembly of Uttar Pradesh is an impressive structure that can compete in architectural style and beauty with perhaps any other construction designed for government use, the members who use it prefer to rip out its furnishings during some of their more violent proceedings, as happened in 1996.

Perhaps a far more serious illustration of Lucknow's urban veering is provided by its geographical features, or their present function. The river Gomti, a curvaceous water body without beauty – once it enters the city limits of Lucknow – is the city's only natural water source and now enjoys the distinction of being the only natural repository for its accumulated waste. The city's real estate industry has never flourished as it does today. It runs on an extensive and complex network of back channels for evaluation, sale, purchase and construction. Most of the builders and contractors (perhaps in some imitation of the traditional practices of the Awadh court) pay a section of their earnings into the coffers of the land mafia as 'obeisance'. Alternatively, mafia-bosses or politicians or indeed those who combine both professional traits may retain ownership of part of the new constructions they have sanctioned, felicitated or legitimized. It is not unlike the criminal dynamics of construction contracts so reminiscent of Bombay in the late 1980s and 1990s.

---

1. *Lucknow: City of Illusion*, The Alkazi Collection of Photography & Prestal Verlag, 2006, p. 8.

Major General Claude Martin the founder of Lucknow's world-renowned public school, La Martiniere College,[2] would perhaps not have felt out of place among the present day elite of political brokers and real estate magnates who breeze in and out of myriad secretariats, hotel lobby's and MLA hostels. Described as, 'an immensely rich man, whose wealth in part was founded on property and the buying, selling and renting of houses in Lucknow,'[3] Martin was a member of the early European set at the Awadh court and his fortunes rested on a combination of militarism, brokering and personal access to the king. Latter day Martins in Lucknow are no less enterprising than their French-Awadhi forerunner (though undoubtedly their social graces do not bear resemblance). Today, neither conscientious staff members of public school institutions trying to counter campus politics nor charming society hostesses objecting to the verbal molestations of criminal youth may confront the rising tide of crime without losing their lives.

Significantly, for the young of Lucknow, whether literate or half-educated, one of the most popular career paths on offer is entry into the Indian Administrative Service (IAS) or other corners of state officialdom. Not in Lucknow the pressing competition of jobs for the IT sector or even call centres. Every vacant space in the city that can hold it advertizes the expert attentions of training centres for entry into the IAS or other government services. Schools operating out of residential colonies run four, sometimes six shifts a day in a bid to prepare the young to fill in the boots left behind by colonial empire-builders.

The advantages are obvious. Nowhere else is the exhibition of the 'perks of power' more evident than in the streets of Lucknow. An inquiry into the ratio of 'VIP vehicles' to ordinary cars in the city will make for an interesting case study, if only to demonstrate the disproportionate allocation of state resources from *Pradesh* to *Pradesh*. While their husbands indulge in the intrigues and counter intrigues of

---

2.   Opened in April 1845.

3.   Rosie Llewellyn-Jones in *Lucknow: City of Illusion*, op cit., p.13.

Lucknow politics, like the *zenana* women or courtiers of old, the wives and families of government officers make full use of their power of patronage and access to ministers, often felicitating or brokering commercial or even governmental transactions.

In his memoirs recalling his stint as the Governor or Uttar Pradesh in 1996, Romesh Bhandari records: 'I soon found out that transfers had in fact become a business. Officers were now accustomed to having their postings changed through powers wielding influence in Raj Bhavan, or with the chief minister when there was a popular government.'[4]

Furthermore, he continues to list the most prized postings and jobs: 'I made my own inquiries and found that there were some clear posts which were greatly in demand. A district magistrate, preferably in one of the important cities, vice chairman or executive officers of development authorities, chief development officers (CDO) in districts, the chief medical officers, and ADM's dealing with finance and revenue. On the side of the police, the post (sic) of SSP or SP in charge of a district was the most prized one.

'As one can see in all these posts, there is great power and patronage. Large expenditures are controlled by these officers. The pattern was that for a posting, the "patron" would be either given a down payment, promises of favours to be done, or in some cases monthly doles.'[5]

The reason it was necessary to cite that particular quote so extensively is that there is perhaps no other official observation on record that is so candid and forthcoming in its assessment of the 'system' and how it works in Uttar Pradesh, and therefore in Lucknow.

And so the 'New Triad' prospers, its membership circulating between the realms of crime, politics and commerce, infecting every sphere of public life in Lucknow. Each member brings with him

---

4.   Romesh Bhandari, *As I Saw It*, Har-Anand Publications, 1998.

5.   Ibid.

dependants and thus more migrants awaiting their chance to carve out their share, to have their slice of Lucknow, as it is, without its historical accoutrements, without the complicated references to tehzib and adab. Each migrant comes to Lucknow on the shoulders of a preceding migrant – that used to be the way in which all great cities grew. Unlike those other cities, civilizations in themselves, Lucknow does not have the energy to mould its inhabitants into its own culture. Instead, it has allowed them to shape her, style her and deface her.

When Nawab Asaf-ud-Daula moved his capital from Faizabad to Lucknow in 1775, he did so with the view of recreating a new empire, borrowing from the old Mughal and infusing into it the innovations of Europe and the West. Architecturally he partly succeeded. Yet within a span of 80 years, Awadh (Oudh) had been annexed by the East India Company and its capital Lucknow reduced to virtual rubble. The consequence of 19th-century courtly decadence was the loss of a fledgling empire. The consequence of 20th-century public apathy, for Lucknow, is the reason it is destined for mediocrity.